THE ART OF WOODWORKING

SHAKER FURNITURE

THE ART OF WOODWORKING

SHAKER FURNITURE

TIME-LIFE BOOKS
ALEXANDRIA, VIRGINIA

ST. REMY PRESS
MONTREAL • NEW YORK

THE ART OF WOODWORKING was produced by
ST. REMY PRESS

PUBLISHER	Kenneth Winchester
PRESIDENT	Pierre Léveillé
Series Editor	Pierre Home-Douglas
Series Art Director	Francine Lemieux
Senior Editor	Marc Cassini
Editor	Andrew Jones
Art Directors	Normand Boudreault,
	Jean-Pierre Bourgeois,
	Michel Giguère
Designers	Hélène Dion, Jean-Guy Doiron,
	François Daxhelet
Picture Editor	Christopher Jackson
Writers	John Dowling, Adam Van Sertima
Contributing Writer	June Sprigg
Contributing Illustrators	Gilles Beauchemin, Michel Blais,
	Ronald Durepos, Michael Stockdale,
	James Thérien
Administrator	Natalie Watanabe
Production Manager	Michelle Turbide
Coordinator	Dominique Gagné
System Coordinator	Eric Beaulieu
Photographer	Robert Chartier
Indexer	Christine M. Jacobs

Time-Life Books is a division of Time Life Inc.,
a wholly owned subsidiary of
THE TIME INC. BOOK COMPANY

TIME-LIFE INC.

President and CEO	John M. Fahey
Editor-in-Chief	John L. Papanek

TIME-LIFE BOOKS

President	John D. Hall
Vice-President, Director of Marketing	Nancy K. Jones
Managing Editor	Roberta Conlan
Director of Design	Michael Hentges
Director of Editorial Operations	Ellen Robling
Consulting Editor	John R. Sullivan
Vice-President, Book Production	Marjann Caldwell
Production Manager	Marlene Zack
Quality Assurance Manager	James King

THE CONSULTANTS

Ian Ingersoll owns a cabinetmaking shop in West Cornwall, Connecticut, that specializes in Shaker furniture.

Giles Miller-Mead taught advanced cabinetmaking at Montreal technical schools for more than ten years. A native of New Zealand, he has worked as a restorer of antique furniture.

Shaker Furniture.
  p. cm. — (The art of woodworking)
Includes index.
ISBN 0-8094-9533-3
1. Furniture making—Amateurs' manuals.
2. Furniture, Shaker—Amateurs' manuals.
I. Time-Life Books.
II. Series.
TT195.S48 1995
749.213'08'8288—dc20   95-1022
                                      CIP

For information about any Time-Life book,
please call 1-800-621-7026, or write:
Reader Information
Time-Life Customer Service
P.O. Box C-32068
Richmond, Virginia
23261-2068

CONTENTS

David Lamb on
REDEFINING SHAKER STYLE

I was fortunate enough to live at the Canterbury Shaker Village in New Hampshire for 14 years, from 1972 to 1986. My parents ran the Village Museum and we were given housing in the Children's House, built in 1810. I had the privilege of knowing seven Shaker Sisters and listened to their beliefs and memories of the old days. While living there, I found myself exploring and studying the architectural elements of the buildings, as well as the furniture in the collections.

While living in these unique surroundings, I had the exceptional opportunity of apprenticing with an Old World cabinetmaker from Madrid, Alejandro de la Cruz. His teachings emphasized tradition, classicism, and integrity in work, design, and living. This apprenticeship provided me with a direction and focus for studying Shaker and other classic designs. At the same time, it allowed me to constructively criticize some old pieces and to rebuild or redesign them by using better construction methods, while still retaining their original charm and attractiveness.

Like the architectural elements of antiquity, the beauty and truth of Shaker design are most evident in basic forms. The overall lines, proportions, and stance can be seen in a simple piece of furniture like the candle stand shown in the photo at right. Details, if they are done well, add a further dimension and will not obscure or clutter the general form.

I do not believe that the Shakers set out to develop their own designs; rather, their beliefs reshaped forms with which they were already familiar. Shaker design can be seen as a stripped-down Federal style, with emphasis on Hepplewhite and Sheraton elements. Federal style was concurrent with the beginning and the development of the Shaker religious movement. The key cabinetmakers of each Shaker village were also free to develop the unique flavor of each community's work while taking direction from the lead community of Mount Lebanon, New York.

While a good deal of Shaker design charm lies in its naiveté, even more depends on the cabinetmaker's complete mastery of the form. Creating furniture designs requires a thorough understanding of the design process, and being able to "get into the heads" of the old masters to understand why certain design decisions were made. It also requires a good understanding of furniture construction using past and present techniques. It is important not just to acknowledge a piece as a masterpiece and copy it, but to find out *why* it is a masterpiece, by asking many questions about it. The answers will provide your building blocks for creating your own designs in any style.

David Lamb was resident cabinetmaker at Canterbury Shaker Village, New Hampshire, between 1979 and 1986. He now builds Shaker-inspired furniture at his shop in Canterbury.

John Wilson perfects the
ELEGANT SHAKER BOX

I first saw Shaker boxes in a pattern book on Shaker woodenware by Ejner Handberg in 1977 when I was teaching furniture making at Lansing Community College. Even as line drawings, these simple, elegant oval containers, crafted from cherry in graduated sizes, were intriguing. All boxes hold universal appeal, but to have them nest inside each other appeals to the child in all of us.

Up to this point, I had been a carpenter in residential construction for 10 years, and had spent another decade teaching social anthropology. Little did I know when I began to follow my curiosity in Shaker oval boxes that they would become the perfect avenue for expressing those three skills—working in wood, interpreting other communities' life and work, and teaching. But that is exactly what has happened to me over the last 15 years.

By specializing in Shaker oval boxes, I was fortunate to take advantage of three trends: a growing awareness of Shaker design, the popularity of woodworking as a hobby, and an interest in instruction in leisure activities. This combination opened the doors for freelance box-making seminars. By 1986 I was teaching 30 workshops a year in many parts of the country, as well as in Canada and England. The participants make a nest of five boxes. It is fulfilling to be able to master the technique of making a box, and even more so to perfect it in making five. In the 12 years since the first box class, I have taught more than 4,000 people this traditional craft.

My memory of first attempting to build them is of bands breaking, bringing the project to an abrupt end. It takes more than line drawings to master technique. Visiting Shaker sites in New England, I recall a rare opportunity to watch box maker Jerry Grant at Hancock Shaker Village. He gave me a sample of the tiny copper tacks that are the hallmark of the box lap. These are as scarce as hen's teeth, as the expression goes. At the time, Cross Nail Company was the one remaining tack manufacturer, and made them only on special order. It took a minimum of 50 pounds to order, and with over 750 tacks to the ounce, that was an incredible supply. With 12 tacks needed to make a box, it also represented a lifetime of box making.

Today, Shaker boxes have become my life and supplying the box trade with quality materials now occupies more of my time than either making boxes or teaching. More than just being good business, making Shaker boxes has left me with the conviction that passing on our skills is a responsibility each of us must accept.

John Wilson taught social anthropology at Purdue before turning his attention to teaching Shaker box making full time in 1983. His seminars have been held at the Smithsonian, in Shaker villages throughout America, and in England. He owns and operates The Home Shop on East Broadway Highway in Charlotte, Michigan.

June Sprigg reflects on
A SHAKER LIFE

W hen I was little and shared a room with my sister, I yearned to have a room of my own. I was 19 when that dream came true, and oh, what a room it was, in an early 19th-Century Shaker building in Canterbury, New Hampshire.

My room was a classic Shaker interior, with built-in cupboards and drawers, a peg rail around the walls, and rare sliding shutters. Everything overhead and underfoot was the work of Shaker Brothers who had used local pine, maple, and birch and a combination of hand tools and water-powered machinery in an efficient and sophisticated system of man-made ponds and mills behind the village. After a century and a half of continual use, the pegs were firm in their sockets. The drawers slid smoothly with a slight tug on the single center pull. The whole effect was one of spaciousness, airiness, and lightness. This room was worth the wait.

By the time I arrived at Canterbury in 1972 as a summer guide in the museum, the Shaker Society had long since flourished and faded. The Canterbury Shakers were established in 1792 as the seventh of what became 19 principal settlements in America. When I came, the half-dozen Shakers who lived there— all in their 70s, 80s, and 90s—were one of the last two Shaker families in existence. (The other was Sabbathday Lake in Maine.) The Sisters were delightful—energetic, humorous, and unstintingly kind. There were no Brothers at Canterbury. The last one had died in the 1930s and the women joked that they had "worked those poor men to death."

While woodworking had passed into history with the last of the Brothers, the Sisters held the work of the "old Shakers" in high regard. A lifetime of using Shaker desks, tables, work counters, chairs, and cupboards had given them a hands-on appreciation of the qualities that have earned Shaker design respect worldwide: strength, lightness, and a simple rightness of proportion. Ergonomic? You bet. We held our breath whenever the fragile but unstoppable Eldress went up and down the stairs with her bad knee and cane, but the breadth of the steps, the gentle rise, and the sturdy, elegant handrail kept her upright and safe.

"Hands to work and hearts to God," a homily of Shaker founder Mother Ann Lee, was a road map for good life. My Shaker friends are gone now, but their work endures as testimony to the beauty and wisdom of that simple message.

June Sprigg has been studying the Shakers for most of her life, and she was Curator of Collections at Hancock Shaker Village between 1979 and 1994. Her latest book with photographer Paul Rocheleau, Shaker Built, *is published by Monacelli Press. She lives in Pittsfield, Massachusetts.*

SHAKER DESIGN

The Shakers are recognized today as one of America's most interesting communal religious societies. Thanks to the vigorous crop of books, articles, and exhibitions that have sprouted up since the Shakers' bicentennial celebration in 1974, most people think of them first and foremost as producers of simple and well-made furniture. But in their heyday from 1825 to 1845, they were better known for their original blend of celibacy and communalism, a deep commitment to Christian principles as practiced by Christ's disciples, and a worship service unique in civilized America for its group dancing, a sort of sacred line or circle dance that gave all members equal opportunity to express the Holy Spirit. This ecstatic dance scandalized many conventional observers, including Ralph Waldo Emerson and Charles Dickens.

With its backward-leaning rear legs and curved slats, the Enfield side chair shown at left was built for simplicity and comfort. The rush seats on early Shaker chairs like this one gradually gave way to canvas tape seating.

By the mid-19th Century, when the lithograph shown above was made, the frenetic dancing that once marked Shaker worship—and gave them their name —had been replaced with more reserved line dances. As in all Shaker activities, the sexes were strictly divided. The woman in stylish Victorian dress in the foreground was probably invited by the Shakers to observe their worship.

The dining hall at the Pleasant Hill community in Harrodsburg, Kentucky.

Mother Ann's New Order

The Shakers trace their history in America to 1774, when founder "Mother Ann" Lee emigrated to New York from Manchester, England, with eight followers. The 39-year-old daughter of a Midlands blacksmith, Ann Lee was prompted to come to the North American colonies, according to her faithful believers, by a vision of the second coming of Christ. She was sickened by the corruption of the Old World, and the changes wrought by the Industrial Revolution that were altering the conditions of human life beyond all previous experience. She sought to establish a new order of life in the New World.

As preached by Ann Lee and her followers, Shaker life was one of hardship and self-denial. Being a Shaker meant living a celibate life with no possibility of bearing children, and working selflessly and equally alongside one's Brothers and Sisters. It also meant living in isolation from the outside world, renouncing all private property, and taking solace in the purity of community and prayer.

Although Ann died a scant 10 years after arriving in America and her movement remained relatively small during her lifetime, converts began to join in droves in the years following her death. By 1787, the first large-scale communal Shaker Family had gathered near Albany at New Lebanon, New York. The New Lebanon community was to become the spiritual capital of the Shaker world through the next century. By 1800, missionaries had helped establish a dozen Shaker communities throughout New England, including ones in Enfield, Connecticut; Harvard, Massachusetts; and Canterbury, New Hampshire. By 1825, 19 principal villages were flourishing from Maine to points west in Kentucky and Ohio. In 1840, an estimated 4,000 Shakers were putting their hands to work and hearts to God in America's largest, best known, and only alternative to mainstream life that existed on a truly national scale.

In spite of efforts to attract new converts, the Shakers' numbers began to decline before the end of the Civil War. In 1875, Tyringham, Massachusetts, was the first Shaker community to close officially. In a century that witnessed so many revolutionary changes in American life it proved difficult for the Shakers—who changed so little—to maintain the momentum of their first 70 years. By 1900, the Shakers had dwindled to 2,000 members as Shaker villages closed their doors one by one. Today, just one community survives, at Sabbathday Lake, Maine, where fewer than a dozen members carry on the Shaker traditions.

Harmony of Proportion

The Shakers were not an esthetic movement or a self-conscious school of design. In fact, their furniture, like their architecture and clothing, was derided in its day for an excessively utilitarian lack of style. Today, attracted by the simplicity of their designs, the world has begun to recognize the achievements of Shaker woodworkers, such as the clocks made by Brother Isaac Newton Youngs of New Lebanon, and the sewing desks

The spiritual center of Shaker life, the meeting house, is as modest and unpretentious as any Shaker building.

and rocking chairs of Brother Freegift Wells of Watervliet, New York.

Simplicity is the quintessential hallmark of Shaker design. Compared with the opulent complexity of a Queen Anne highboy, for example, a Shaker chair is a paragon of austerity: four legs, three slats, a handful of stretchers, and a few yards of canvas tape for the seat. In a world that seems to grow increasingly more complex and chaotic year by year it is not difficult to see why the simple, harmonious lines of Shaker furniture continue to hold their appeal.

Shaker artisans also distinguished themselves by the quality of their work. They rarely needed to hurry and were in fact encouraged to take the time needed to do the job properly. The communal family structure gave individuals freedom from thoughts of purchasing, marketing, sales, and all related business concerns—an experienced business staff took care of all that. Shaker woodworkers received free training from very fine craftsmen, older Brothers who taught them in an apprenticeship system. Shakers generally worked in big, handsome, state-of-the-art workshops with the best tools and machines available; a communal economy, thrifty living, and an abhorrence of buying on credit usually meant plenty of capital to invest in the best. The Shakers' were also capable of inventing the best; the table saw, for example, was the brainchild of a Shaker sister. It comes as no surprise that many woodworkers today speak enviously at times of their Shaker counterparts.

A Lack of Ornamentation

The religious motivation behind the simplicity of Shaker design is an obvious one. The Shakers sought in every-

thing they did to free themselves from the vain and unnecessary, which to them meant avoiding gross materialism. This was no mean feat in the Gilded Age that gave birth to Victoriana and conspicuous consumption. The Shakers eschewed the

sort of artistic freedom that allowed builders to design and make whatever they wanted. They seldom autographed their pieces because they took no pride in being recognized as individual artisans. Religious convictions also forbade

Brother Charles Greaves outside the carpenty shop, Hancock Shaker Village, Pittsfield, Massachusetts, in the early 1900s.

a license to decorate with carving, inlay, painting, exotic imported woods, or any other type of applied ornament. The Shakers traditionally regarded these embellishments as a waste of time and resources. Indeed, the few ornamental touches to be found on Shaker furniture—such as exposed dovetailing and the ubiquitous, neatly turned drawer pulls and rail pegs—invariably had a utilitarian purpose.

Usually made with bent maple sides and quartersawn pine tops and bottoms, oval boxes were used to store all types of dry goods. They were constructed in graduated sizes so that each one could be stored inside the next larger size.

Believing that all things visible revealed the state of the spirit within, Shakers took great care with what they made so that its near-perfection would both honor and emulate the excellence of God's own creation. Above all else, Shaker furniture and design is imbued with the spirit of its makers, proclaiming their optimism and faith in the future. By spending obvious care and time on humble, useful things, the Shakers clearly announced their belief in a future worth living and in the ability of future generations to keep their craft alive.

On the following pages is an illustrated gallery of some of the most enduring pieces of furniture that serve as the Shakers' legacy to modern woodworking.

A tall clock serves as a boundary between the men's and women's sleeping areas in the Centre Family Dwelling at Pleasant Hill, Kentucky. Clocks also divided the Shakers' daily lives into prescribed segments. There were specific times for rising, eating, working, and sleeping.

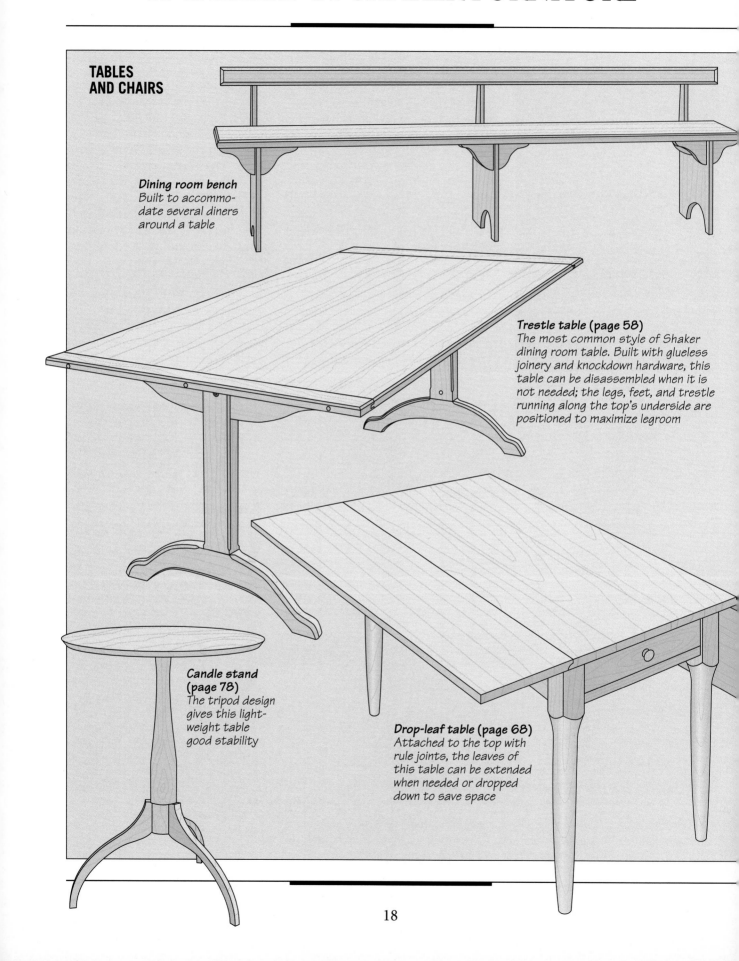

**TABLES
AND CHAIRS**

Dining room bench
*Built to accommo-
date several diners
around a table*

Trestle table (page 58)
*The most common style of Shaker
dining room table. Built with glueless
joinery and knockdown hardware, this
table can be disassembled when it is
not needed; the legs, feet, and trestle
running along the top's underside are
positioned to maximize legroom*

**Candle stand
(page 78)**
*The tripod design
gives this light-
weight table
good stability*

Drop-leaf table (page 68)
*Attached to the top with
rule joints, the leaves of
this table can be extended
when needed or dropped
down to save space*

Revolving chair
Also called swivel stools or revolvers, these chairs were used in Shaker offices, shops, and schoolrooms

Enfield side chair (page 26)
Made with a backward tilt to provide comfort without bending the chair's rear legs. Early versions like the one shown featured rush seats; the Shakers later relied on canvas tape, as in the rocking chair shown at right

Rocking chair (page 38)
Has steam-bent rear legs and solid-wood rockers; the tape seating is available in a variety of colors and patterns. Also made in a ladderback version

Meetinghouse bench
Accommodated the faithful during Shaker religious services; with its solid pine seat, this simple and lightweight chair could be moved out of the way easily when necessary

With their short backs, the splint-seat dining chairs shown above can slide under a table without any sacrifice of comfort.

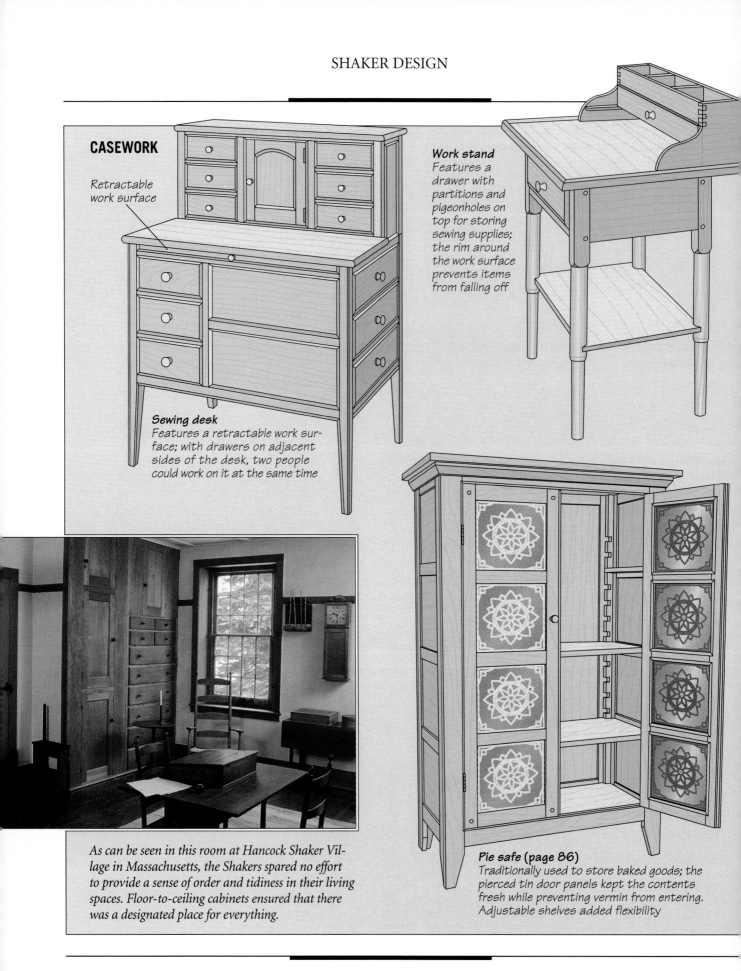

CASEWORK

Retractable work surface

Work stand
Features a drawer with partitions and pigeonholes on top for storing sewing supplies; the rim around the work surface prevents items from falling off

Sewing desk
Features a retractable work surface; with drawers on adjacent sides of the desk, two people could work on it at the same time

As can be seen in this room at Hancock Shaker Village in Massachusetts, the Shakers spared no effort to provide a sense of order and tidiness in their living spaces. Floor-to-ceiling cabinets ensured that there was a designated place for everything.

Pie safe (page 86)
Traditionally used to store baked goods; the pierced tin door panels kept the contents fresh while preventing vermin from entering. Adjustable shelves added flexibility

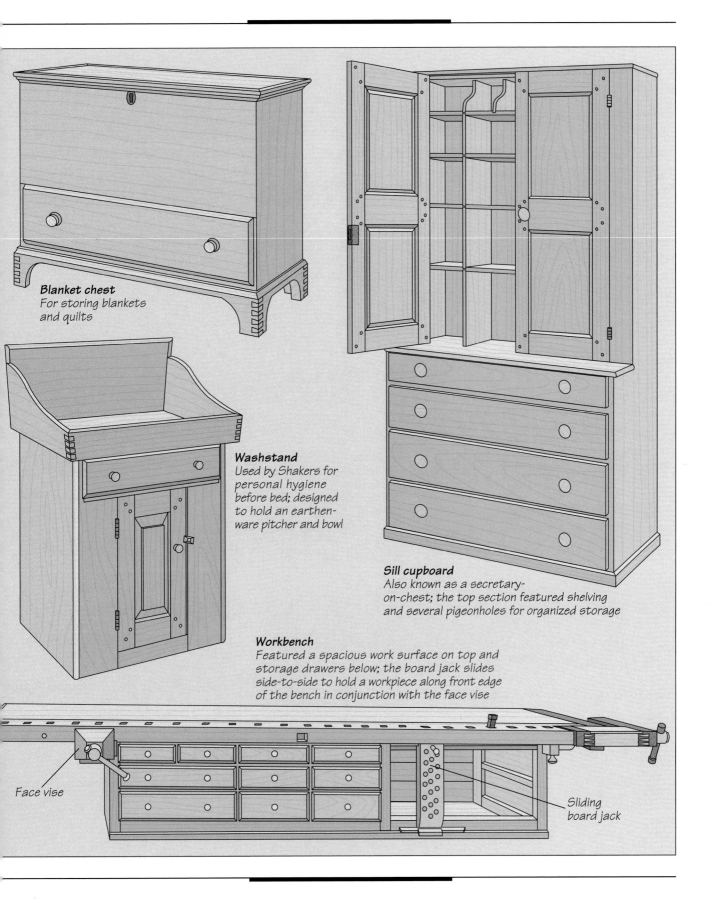

Blanket chest
For storing blankets
and quilts

Washstand
Used by Shakers for
personal hygiene
before bed; designed
to hold an earthen-
ware pitcher and bowl

Sill cupboard
Also known as a secretary-
on-chest; the top section featured shelving
and several pigeonholes for organized storage

Workbench
Featured a spacious work surface on top and
storage drawers below; the board jack slides
side-to-side to hold a workpiece along front edge
of the bench in conjunction with the face vise

Face vise

Sliding
board jack

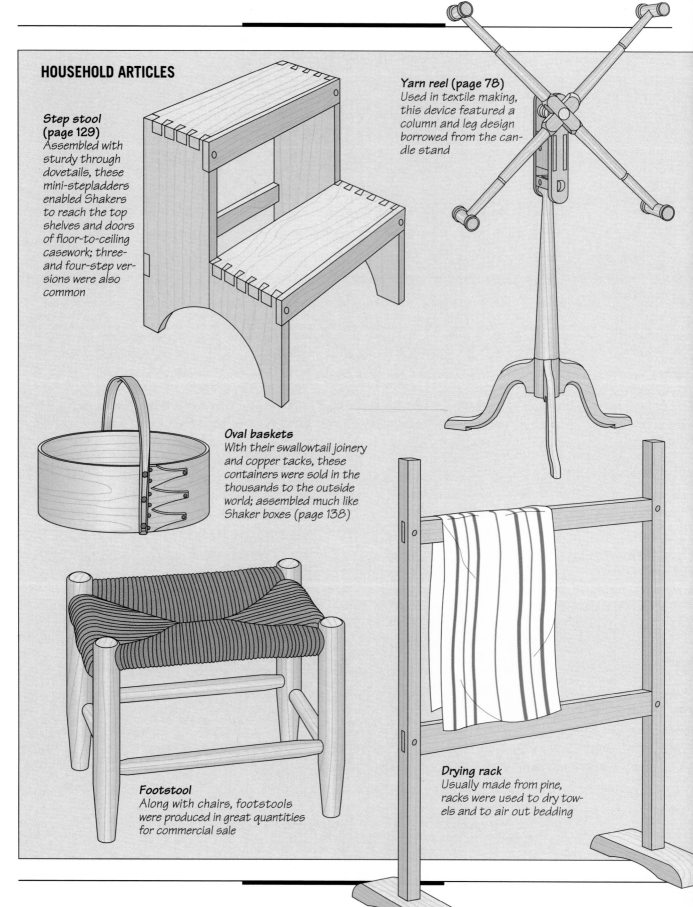

HOUSEHOLD ARTICLES

**Step stool
(page 129)**
Assembled with
sturdy through
dovetails, these
mini-stepladders
enabled Shakers
to reach the top
shelves and doors
of floor-to-ceiling
casework; three-
and four-step ver-
sions were also
common

Yarn reel (page 78)
Used in textile making,
this device featured a
column and leg design
borrowed from the can-
dle stand

Oval baskets
With their swallowtail joinery
and copper tacks, these
containers were sold in the
thousands to the outside
world; assembled much like
Shaker boxes (page 138)

Footstool
Along with chairs, footstools
were produced in great quantities
for commercial sale

Drying rack
Usually made from pine,
racks were used to dry tow-
els and to air out bedding

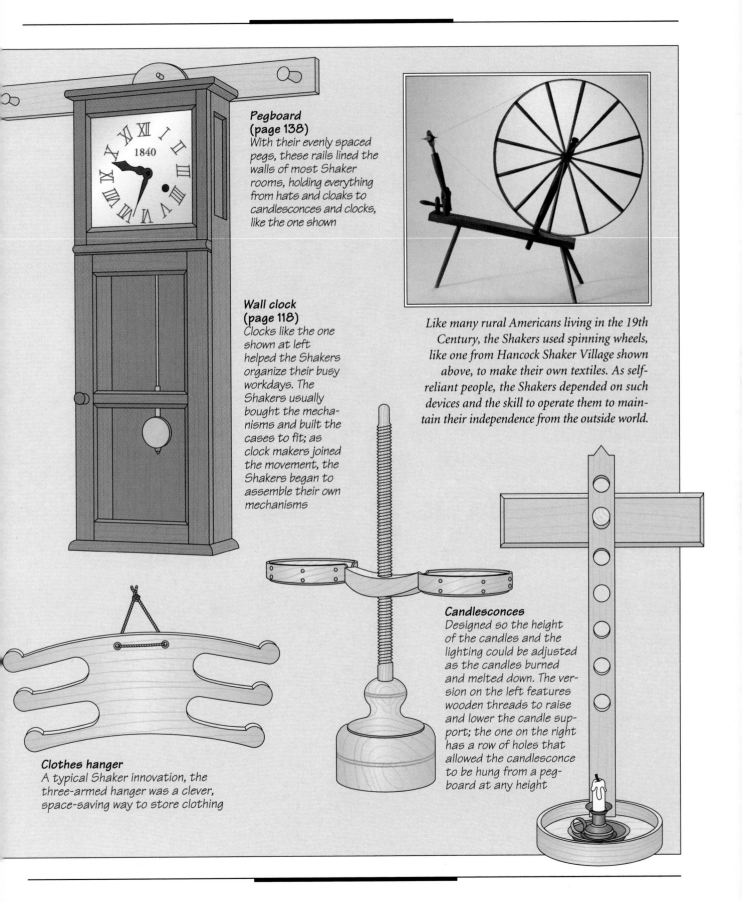

**Pegboard
(page 138)**
With their evenly spaced pegs, these rails lined the walls of most Shaker rooms, holding everything from hats and cloaks to candlesconces and clocks, like the one shown

**Wall clock
(page 118)**
Clocks like the one shown at left helped the Shakers organize their busy workdays. The Shakers usually bought the mechanisms and built the cases to fit; as clock makers joined the movement, the Shakers began to assemble their own mechanisms

Like many rural Americans living in the 19th Century, the Shakers used spinning wheels, like one from Hancock Shaker Village shown above, to make their own textiles. As self-reliant people, the Shakers depended on such devices and the skill to operate them to maintain their independence from the outside world.

Clothes hanger
A typical Shaker innovation, the three-armed hanger was a clever, space-saving way to store clothing

Candlesconces
Designed so the height of the candles and the lighting could be adjusted as the candles burned and melted down. The version on the left features wooden threads to raise and lower the candle support; the one on the right has a row of holes that allowed the candlesconce to be hung from a pegboard at any height

CHAIRS

Anticipating modern-day advertisers by more than 100 years, the Shakers proudly promoted their wares to a marketplace of non-believers who were nevertheless poised to purchase quality furniture. As one of their early catalogs proclaimed, Shaker chairs offered "durability, simplicity, and lightness." The level of craftsmanship that they attained enabled them to back up their claims. Shaker-made chairs sold well, proving that their business acumen was as well developed as their piety.

The Shakers had astutely reasoned that chairs were the right product for the market. First, chairs needed relatively little stock to build—compared to case furniture—so they could be made economically. Furthermore, most models could be built quite quickly, and they were compact and light enough for easy storage and transportation. Finally, chairs are a common household item; most buyers required several. All of these factors enabled their chair-making enterprise to contribute significantly to Shaker prosperity.

This chapter presents step-by-step instructions for building three classic Shaker chairs. The Enfield side chair *(page 26)* features a simple design that belies the fine craftsmanship and precise joinery needed to build it. Its legs, rails, and stretchers are turned on the lathe, and the pieces are connected with

With precisely positioned and sized mortises, the crest rail of the Shaker-style meetinghouse bench shown above is fitted onto the spindles. The Shakers built longer versions of the bench to serve as pews at religious meetings.

mortise-and-tenon joints. The chair back consists of slats that must be steam-bent. A traditional method for forming the chair seat—woven rush—is shown beginning on page 34. The alternative seat style illustrated in the photo at far left, using a tape upholstery material that the Shakers called listing, is explained starting on page 45.

With its turned parts and mortise-and-tenon joinery, the Mt. Lebanon-style rocking chair *(page 38)* shares many features with the Enfield. However, the rear legs of the rocker, which are bent for comfort, and the rockers themselves—fixed to the legs with dowel-reinforced bridle joints—are elegant refinements. The chair is named after the community in upstate New York where prototypes were built.

Despite its traditional use as a pew for religious purposes, the spindle-backed meetinghouse bench has many contemporary applications. The version shown on page 48 features a solid-wood seat with ample room for two or three users.

Each of these chairs—early examples of which are still intact today—embodies the Shaker belief once set forth by Mother Ann, founder of the sect: "Build as though you were to live for a thousand years, and as you would do if you knew you were to die tomorrow."

Blue and white cloth tape, or listing, is being woven between the rear legs of the rocker shown at left, providing a strong, attractive, and lightweight seat back. This rocker was finished with tung oil, then rubbed with blue-tinted beeswax to harmonize with the color of the listing.

ENFIELD SIDE CHAIR

The most striking feature of the Enfield side chair is its backward slant of 98°, as shown in the side view on page 27. The design allows the chair to conform to the anatomy of the typical user and provide comfortable seating without needing steam-bent back posts. The slant, however, does present a challenge in executing the joinery. Few of the joints in this chair are cut square; most are assembled at compound angles. It is a good idea to refer back to the side and top views as you build the chair, using the angles to help set up your drill when boring the round mortises. As a result of the seat's trapezoidal shape, the front legs are spaced farther apart than the rear ones. Also, the rear legs are splayed outward from bottom to top by 2°. Consequently, the back stretchers, seat rail, and slats are progressively longer towards the top of the chair. Refer to the cutting list on page 27 for precise dimensions.

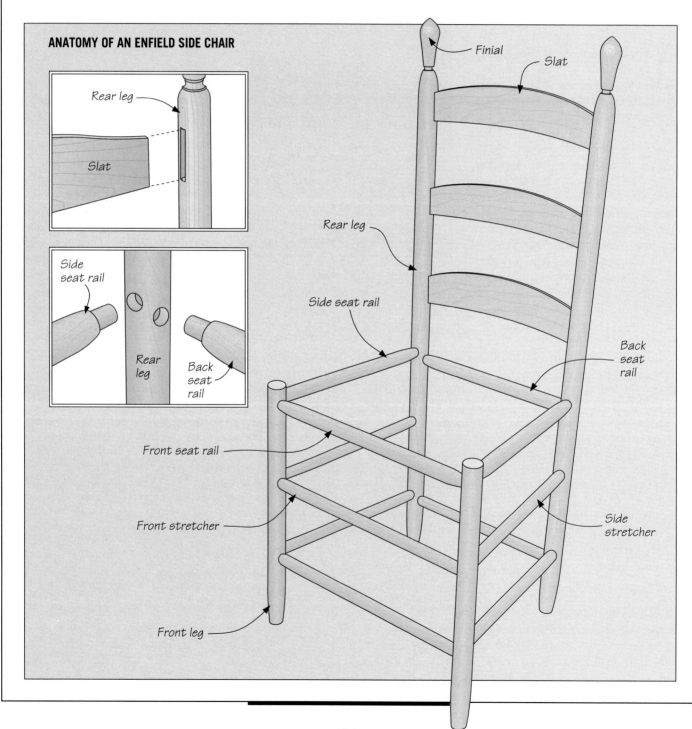

ANATOMY OF AN ENFIELD SIDE CHAIR

Rear leg

Slat

Side seat rail

Rear leg

Back seat rail

Finial

Slat

Rear leg

Side seat rail

Back seat rail

Front seat rail

Front stretcher

Side stretcher

Front leg

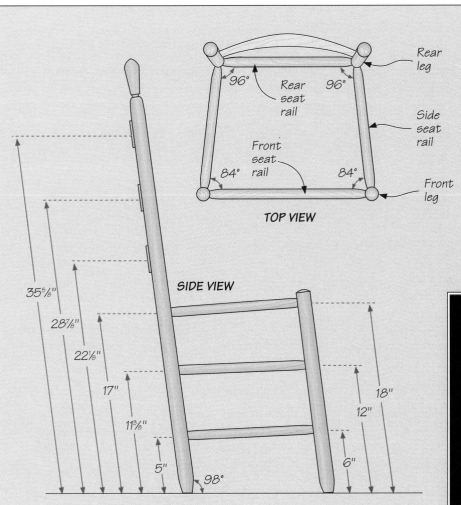

TOP VIEW

SIDE VIEW

As shown in the top view of the side chair *(left, top)*, the front legs are parallel, but the rear ones are angled slightly apart by 2°. The slats are joined to the rear legs at a slight angle. The side view *(left, bottom)* illustrates the chair's backward lean. Although this design feature eliminates the need to bend the rear legs, the joints require careful execution.

The cherry Enfield side chair shown above features a fiber rush seat and a tung oil finish, which combine to create a warm and natural appearance.

ITEM		QTY	L	W OR DIAM.	TH
Legs	Rear	2	41½	1¼	
	Front	2	19¼	1¼	
Seat rail*	Front	1	18½	1	
	Back	1	14½	1	
	Side	2	14	1	
Stretchers*	Front	2	18½	¾	
	Back	1	13¾	¾	
	Side	4	14	¾	
Slats	Top	1	15	2¾	¼
	Middle	1	14¾	2¾	¼
	Bottom	1	14½	2¾	¼

*Note: Measurements include tenon lengths.

PLANNING THE JOB

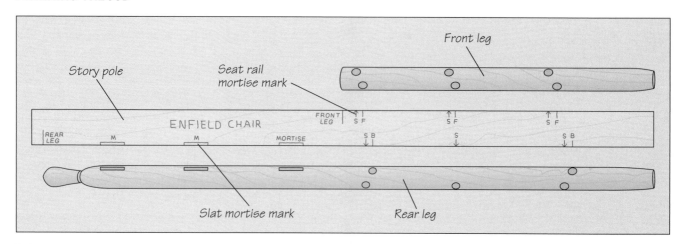

Story pole

Seat rail
mortise mark

Front leg

ENFIELD CHAIR

FRONT
LEG

REAR
LEG   M   M   MORTISE

Slat mortise mark

Rear leg

Using a story pole

To help you size and prepare the chair legs, mark key dimensions and the location of mortises on a shop-made story pole. Made from a strip of plywood, the story pole shown above includes the length of the front and rear legs, and the placement of the stretcher, rail, and slat mortises. Refer to the side view illustration of the Enfield chair on page 27 for the height of each element. The marks on the jig can then be used to cut the leg blanks to length and outline the mortises on the blanks. Note that the mortises for the front or back stretchers or rails are offset ½ inch lower than the mortises for the side ones to avoid weakening the legs. Label the story pole and keep it for future chair-making.

PREPARING THE LEGS, RAILS AND STRETCHERS

1 Routing the slat mortises in the rear legs

Outline the slat mortises on your rear leg blanks using the story pole shown above, centering the outlines on the inside face of each blank. Then secure one of the blanks between bench dogs. Install a ¼-inch mortising bit in a router equipped with an edge guide. Center the bit over the mortise outline and adjust the edge guide to butt against the stock; use the second leg blank to support the router. Make several passes, increasing the cutting depth with each pass until the mortise is completed to a depth of ⅝ inch. Repeat to rout the remaining mortises in both blanks *(right)*, then square the corners of the cavities with a chisel.

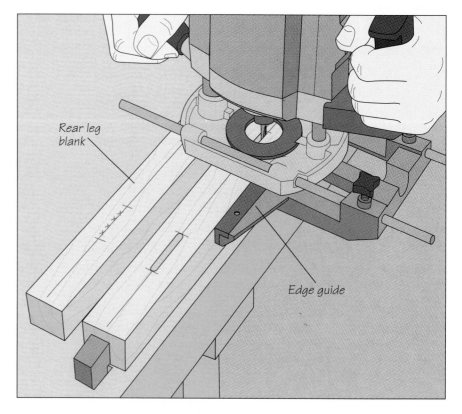

Rear leg
blank

Edge guide

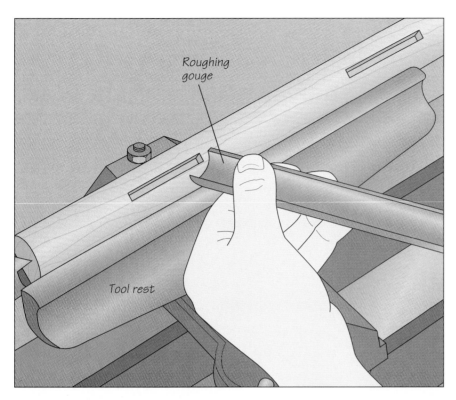

Roughing gouge

Tool rest

2 Turning the rear legs
Place a rear leg blank between centers on your lathe, position the tool rest as close as possible to the workpiece without touching it, and turn on the machine. Supporting a roughing gouge on the tool rest, carefully move the bevel until it touches the blank and the cutting edge starts removing waste. Continue working all along the length of the blank until you form a cylinder *(left)*, with the bevel rubbing and the tool pointing in the direction of the cut.

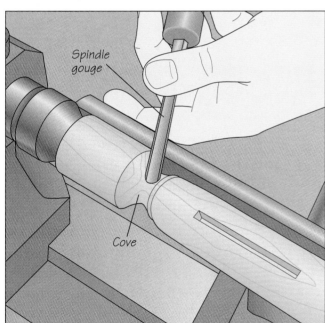

Spindle gouge

Cove

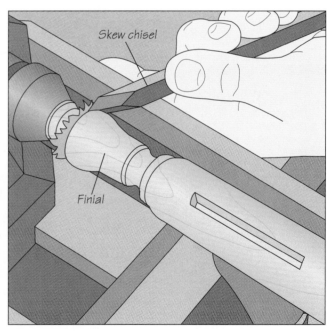

Skew chisel

Finial

3 Turning the finials on the rear legs
Start by cutting the cove that separates the finial from the cylindrical section of the leg. Use a roughing gouge at first, then switch to a spindle gouge. Holding the tool in an underhand grip and rubbing the bevel on the stock, slice into the wood and make a scooping cut down the middle of the cove *(above, left)*. Switch to a skew chisel to shape the finial. Set the blade on the tool rest and advance it until it cuts into the stock. Shape the finial as desired, making sure the bevel is rubbing throughout the cut *(above, right)*. Use sandpaper to shape the tip. Turn the other rear leg and its finial the same way.

4 Turning the rails and stretchers

Turn the rails and stretchers as you did the rear legs *(page 29)*, using a parting tool to cut the tenons at the ends of each piece *(right)*. Ensure a snug fit by making the diameter of the tenons equal to that of the bit you will use to bore the mortises *(page 31)*. The tenon length should be one-half the thickness of the legs. Finally, turn the front legs.

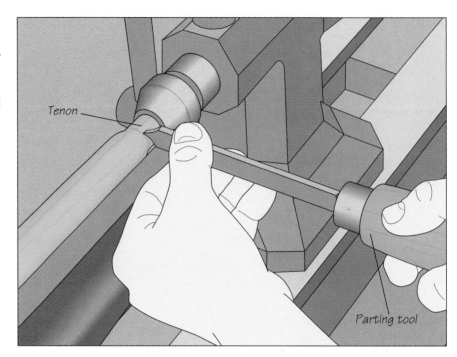

Tenon

Parting tool

MAKING THE SLATS

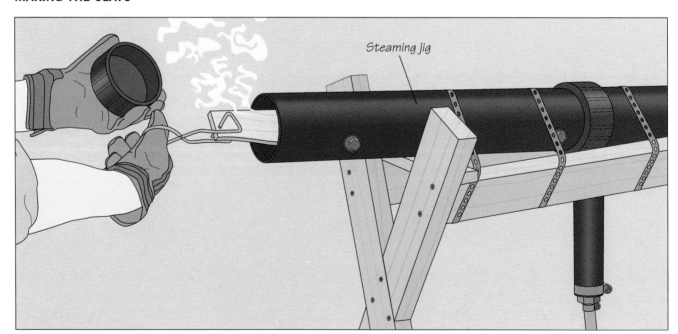

Steaming jig

1 Steaming the slats

Set up a steaming jig, referring to the back endpaper for construction details. Also have a bending jig ready *(step 2)*. Turn on the steam source and mark the center of each slat. Once steam begins to escape from the jig's drain hole, place a slat inside. Close the end cap tightly and let the wood steam until it is soft. As a rough guide, steam air-dried lumber for one hour per inch of thickness; half that time for green wood. Avoid scalding your hands by wearing work gloves and using tongs to handle the stock *(above)*. Place the next slat in the jig and bend the steamed slat without delay.

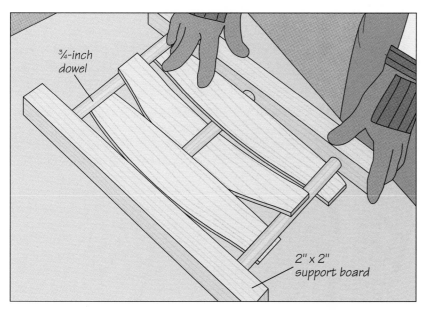

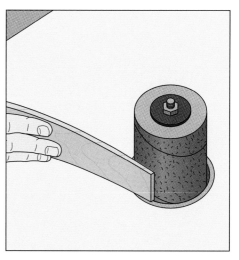

2 Bending the slats

To make the bending form shown above, center the mortises for the dowels along the length of the support boards. The distance between the two outside dowels should be slightly less than the span of a slat when it is curved. As soon as you remove a slat from the steamer, quickly fit it between the dowels. Center the slats against the middle dowel and push the ends behind the outside dowels. Alternate the direction of the slats to equalize pressure on the jig.

3 Preparing the slats for their mortises

Let the slats dry in the bending form for a couple of days, then test-fit them in the rear legs and cut them to length. For a snug fit, sand the ends of the slats on a spindle shaper. Carefully sand down the part of the back face that will fit into the mortise *(above)*; check the fit periodically as you go. A gouge can also be used to cut away waste until you have a good fit.

PREPARING THE LEGS FOR THE RAILS AND STRETCHERS

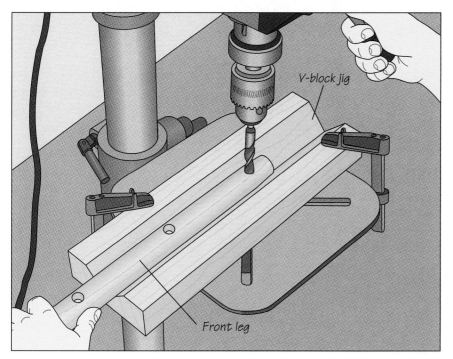

1 Preparing the front legs for the front rails and stretchers

The only round mortises in the Enfield chair that are drilled at 90° are those in the front legs for the front rails and stretchers. Use your story pole *(page 28)* to outline the hole locations on the front legs and bore them on your drill press. Cut a V-shaped wedge out of a wood block, creating a jig that will cradle the legs as you drill the holes. Install a bit the same diameter as the rail and stretcher tenons, and clamp the jig to the machine table so the bottom of the V is centered under the bit. Then place the leg in the jig and set the drilling depth to slightly more than the tenon length—about two-thirds the stock diameter. Holding the leg with one hand, bore the mortises *(left)*. Repeat for the other front leg.

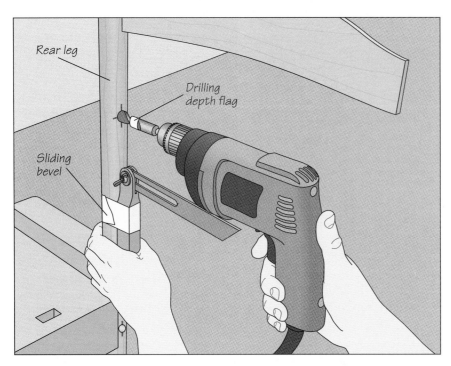

2 Preparing the rear legs for the back rails and stretchers

The mortises in the rear legs for the back rails and stretchers must be angled down by 2° to compensate for the slight splaying out of the back legs. Set one of the legs upright in a bench vise, making sure it is vertical. Use a protractor to adjust a sliding bevel to 92°. Wrap a strip of masking tape around the bit to mark the drilling depth—about two-thirds the leg diameter. To help you hold the drill at the correct angle as you bore the hole, tape the handle of the sliding bevel to the leg and keep the bit parallel to the blade of the tool. Stop drilling once the depth flag contacts the stock. Repeat the process to drill the remaining holes in both legs *(left)*, repositioning the leg in the vise and the sliding bevel on the leg as necessary.

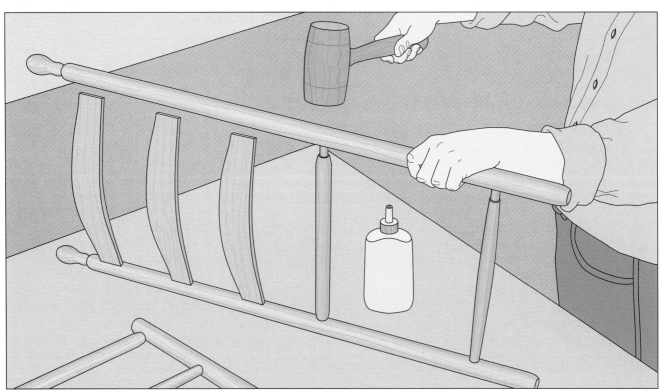

3 Gluing the front and back rails, stretchers, and slats to the legs

Before drilling the holes in the legs for the side rails and stretchers, assemble the front legs and then the rear legs. Starting with the front legs, spread glue on the rail and stretcher tenons and in the leg mortises and fit the pieces together. Tap the joints into final position with a wooden mallet. Repeat for the rear legs, gluing the slats in place as well *(above)*.

4 Preparing the legs for the side rails and stretchers

The mortises in the legs for the side rails and stretchers must be drilled at compound angles—they are angled in both the horizontal and vertical planes. Start by securing one of the rear legs in a handscrew and clamping the assembly upright to a work surface. Then use the chair seat and side views on page 27, a protractor, and a sliding bevel to determine the drilling angle as you did in step 2. But instead of taping two sliding bevels to the stock, cut two square pieces of plywood, clamping one to the leg to indicate the vertical angle and the second to the rail or stretcher for the horizontal angle. For each hole, align the bit with the top edge of the vertical guide (labeled SIDE in the illustration) and the side edge of the horizontal guide (labeled TOP) *(right)*. Again, stop drilling when the drilling depth flag contacts the stock. Using similar methods, drill the front leg assembly.

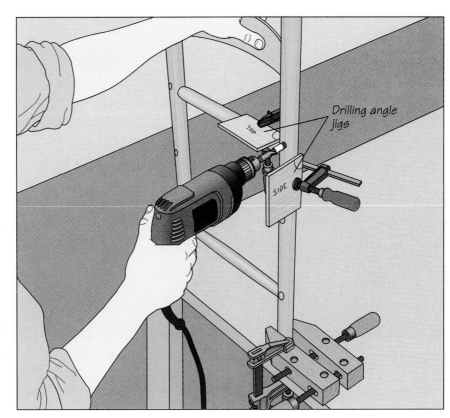

Drilling angle jigs

ASSEMBLING THE CHAIR

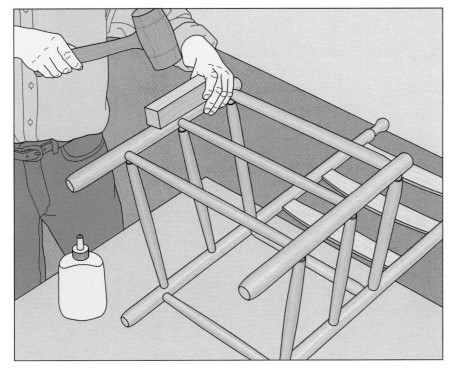

Gluing up the chair

Once all the mortises are drilled, spread glue on the tenons of the side rails and stretchers and in the mortises, and fit the pieces together. Use a wooden mallet and a wood block to tap all the joints into final position *(left)*. Then set the chair upright. The four legs should all be flat on the floor. If not, you may have to apply firm but gentle twisting to one or more of the connections to coax the legs into position.

RUSH SEAT

arly Shaker chairs, like the Enfield chair featured on the preceding pages, were finished with rush seats. Traditionally, the rush was natural, consisting of marsh grass twisted into a cord which was woven in a center diamond pattern over the frame. Rush seats are both comfortable and durable, and can be done in an hour and a half or so once you get the knack.

This section shows how to rush a chair seat with a more contemporary material—tough-grade, fiber paper twisted into long strands, known as fiber or manila rush. Craft supply dealers are usually good sources of advice for the appropriate size and amount of rush needed for a particular project. Before starting, spray the individual lengths of rush with water to keep them pliable.

A fiber rush seat is woven onto a Shaker-inspired Enfield chair. Using this traditional material and the simple technique for installing it can impart a charming appearance to any stick-style chair.

RUSHING A CHAIR SEAT

1 Bridging the front rail
Since the rails that form the seat of an Enfield chair do not form a square, you must use rush to create a square seat frame. Measure the difference in length between the front and back seat rails and divide your measurement in half. Measure your result along the front rail from each of the front legs and make a mark on the rail. Tack a length of slightly dampened rushing that is about twice the length of the front rail to the inside of a side rail about 2 inches from the front leg. Loop the rush around the front rail from underneath, then around the side rail from underneath. Bring the rush across the front rail and loop it around the other side rail and the front rail in the same manner *(right)*. Holding the rush taut, tack it to the side rail opposite the first tack.

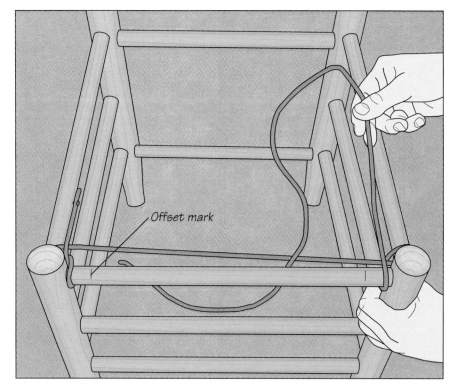

Offset mark

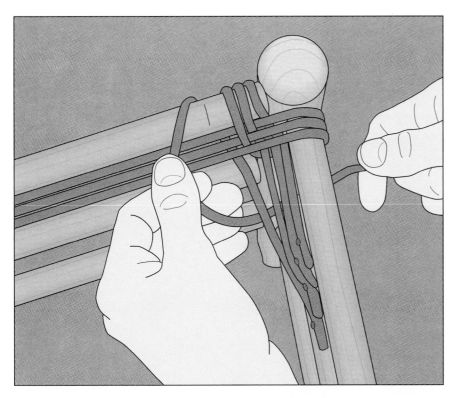

2 Squaring the seat frame
Fasten a length of rush alongside the first one, using the technique described in step 1. Loop it around the front and side rails, like the first strands, and fasten it to the opposite rail. Continue adding lengths of rush *(left)* until you reach the offset marks you made on the front rail. Be sure to keep the rush as tight and straight as possible.

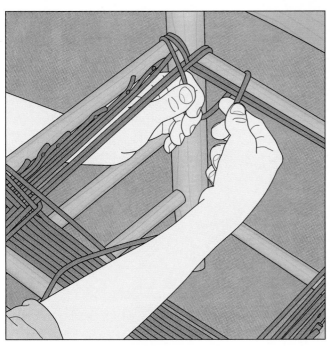

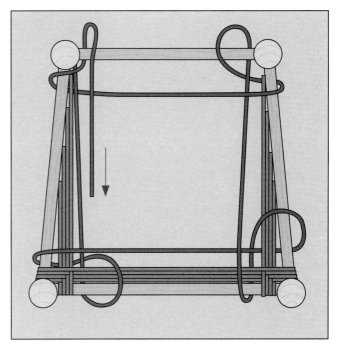

3 Weaving a complete circuit
Once you have squared the seat frame, you can begin rushing the seat all around the frame. Working with an approximately 20-foot length of rush, tack it to the side rail near the rear legs and loop it around all the rails *(above, left)*. Keep working around the chair using the same pattern *(above, right)*. When you get to the end of a length of rush, clamp it temporarily to the seat frame to keep it taut and attach it to a new piece using a figure eight knot. Locate the knots on the underside of the seat so they will not be visible.

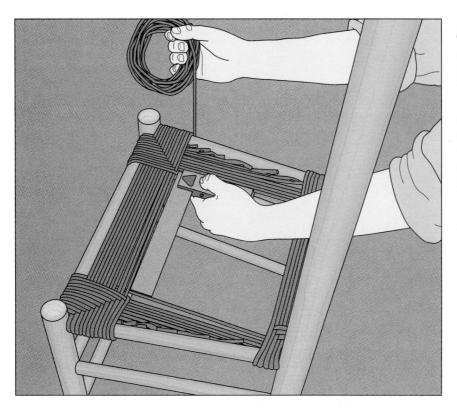

4 Checking the weave for square
Once every third or fourth circuit, check whether the sides of the seat are perpendicular to each other. Holding the length of rush in a coil with one hand, butt a try square in one corner of the seat *(left)*. The handle and blade of the square should rest flush against the rushing. If not, use a flat-tip screwdriver to straighten the side that is out-of-square, pushing the last circuit you installed against the adjacent ones. Repeat at the remaining corners of the seat.

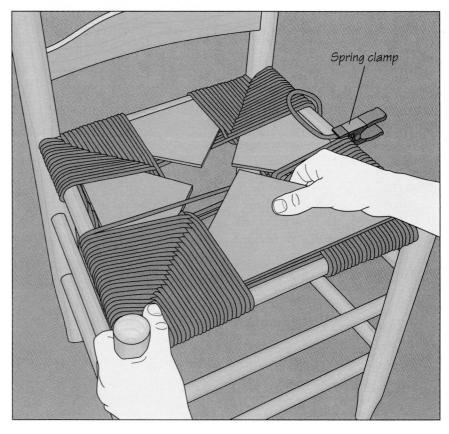

Spring clamp

5 Stuffing the seat
Once the rushing is about two-thirds done, it is time to provide extra padding by stuffing the seat. To prevent the rush from slackening, use a spring clamp to secure the loose length you are installing to a seat rail. Use cardboard for the padding, cutting one triangular piece for each side of the seat so that the triangle's long side is slightly shorter than the seat rail. Slip the padding under the rushing *(right)*, then trim the tips if they overlap in the center. Continue the normal circuit as before until the two side rails are covered.

6 Completing the bridge

Since the seat on an Enfield chair is deeper than it is wide, the rushing being installed on the side rails will meet in the middle of the seat before the rush on the front and back rails. Once this occurs, use a technique known as bridging to fill the gap. Loop the rushing on the front and back rails with a figure-eight pattern weave, passing the rush over the back rail, down through the center, under the seat and up around the front rail. Then bring the rush over the seat from the front rail and back down through the center *(right)*. Pass the rush under the seat, come up around the back rail again and repeat the procedure.

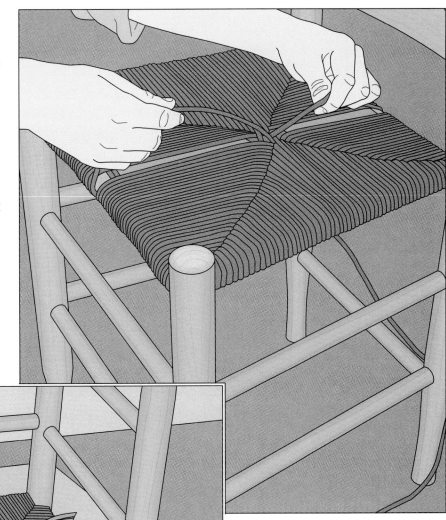

7 Finishing the job

Once you have bridged the gap between the front and back rails, set the chair upside down on a work table and tack the last strand of rush to the under-side of the back seat rail *(left)*. Cut off the excess.

SHAKER ROCKING CHAIR

The Shaker rocker shown below shares many features and building techniques with the Enfield side chair. For example, the crest rail mortises in the rear legs are routed *(page 28)* before the legs are turned and bent. (In this chair, the rear legs are bent from the arms to the top, instead of being canted back, as on the Enfield.) The mortises for the back stretchers, rail, and slats are then bored with an electric drill *(page 32)*; the mortises must be angled 2° to compensate for the outward splay of the legs from the bottom to the top.

Drilling the mortises in the legs for the other stretchers and rails is simpler because there are no holes at compound angles. The mortises for the front rails and stretchers are 90° holes that can be bored on the drill press *(page 31)*. The mortises for the side rails and stretchers can be bored with a drill and shop-made drilling guides *(page 33)*; adjust the "TOP" guide to the appropriate angle, and set up the "SIDE" guide at 90°.

The following pages present techniques that are unique to building a Shaker rocker, including bending the rear legs *(page 40)*, and making the arms and rockers *(page 41)*.

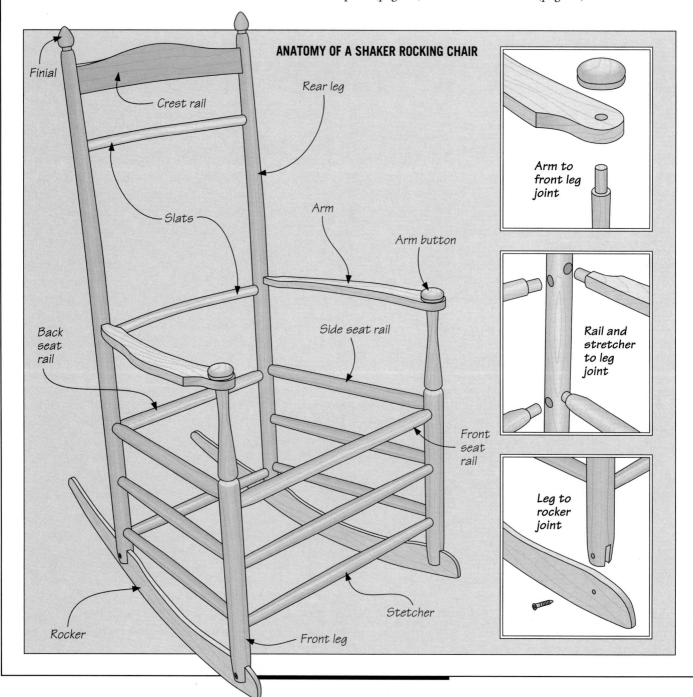

ANATOMY OF A SHAKER ROCKING CHAIR

Finial

Crest rail

Rear leg

Slats

Arm

Arm button

Back seat rail

Side seat rail

Front seat rail

Rocker

Stetcher

Front leg

Arm to front leg joint

Rail and stretcher to leg joint

Leg to rocker joint

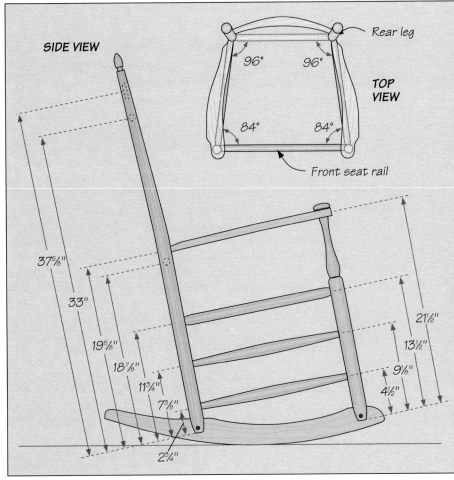

SIDE VIEW

Rear leg

96° 96°

TOP VIEW

84° 84°

Front seat rail

37⅝"

33"

19⅝"

18⅞"

11¾"

7⅞"

2¾"

21½"

13½"

9⅛"

4½"

As shown in the overhead view of the rocking chair *(left, top)*, the front of the seat is wider than the back and the tops of the rear legs are farther apart at the top than the bottom. As a result, the rails and slats are progressively longer from the bottom to the top of the chair. Like the rear legs, the slats are steam-bent for comfort. The front legs are parallel so the front rails and stretchers all share the same length.

As shown in the side view *(left, bottom)*, the side rails and stretchers are perpendicular to the legs in the vertical axis. A comfortable angle is achieved by bending the rear legs, rather than inclining them. For balance, the rockers contact the ground 2 to 3 inches in front of the rear legs. The illustrations and cutting list provide appropriate dimensions and angles that you can transfer to your story pole *(page 28)*.

Built in Hancock Shaker Village, the rocker shown above features a woven-splint seat. The Shakers made this seating from wood, which they soaked in water for several weeks, then split into long strips and wove around the seat rails.

ITEM		QTY	L	W OR DIAM.	TH
Legs	front*	2	22½	1½	
	rear	2	41½	1½	
Seat rails*	front	1	22	1	
	back	1	17½	1	
	side	2	18½	1	
Stretchers*	front	2	22	¾	
	back	1	17	¾	
	side	4	18½	¾	
Arms		2	19	3½	⅜
Rockers		2	31	5	⅜
Slats*	top	1	18	¾	
	bottom	1	17½	¾	
Crest rail		1	18½	3	¼

*Notes: Dimensions include tenon lengths.

PREPARING THE REAR LEGS

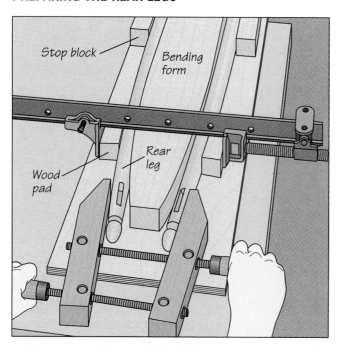

1 Bending the legs

Rout the crest rail mortises in the rear legs (page 28), turn them on your lathe (page 29), then steam the legs (page 30) for bending. To bend them to the proper arc, use a shop-made jig, like the one shown at left. For the jig base, cut a piece of plywood longer than the legs, then make the bending form from a piece of solid stock slightly thicker than the leg diameter. On your band saw, cut the desired curve—about 10°—on both edges of the form, starting the cut about halfway up the board. Then screw the form to the base and fasten a stop block on each side of the straight portion of the form; the gap between the blocks and the form should equal the leg diameter. As soon as you take the legs from the steamer, set them on the jig between the form and the blocks, aligning the point on the legs that will be joined to the seat rails with the start of the curved cut on the form. Then, protecting the stock with wood pads, install a bar clamp just below the slat mortises to bend the legs snugly against the form. Secure the top of the legs against the form using a handscrew *(left)*.

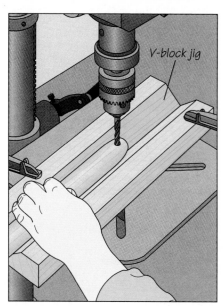

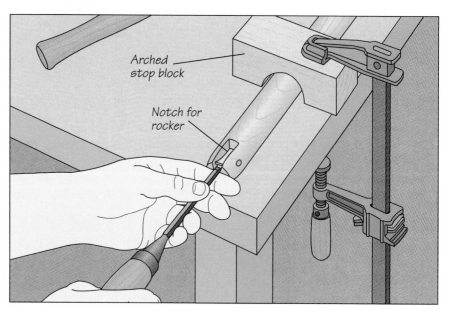

2 Preparing the legs for the rockers

Once the legs are dry, mark holes for the screws that will fasten the legs to the rockers; locate a hole on each leg about 1 inch from the bottom end. Cut a V-shaped wedge out of a wood block, creating a jig that will hold the legs as you bore the holes. Clamp the jig to your drill press table so the bottom of the V is centered under the bit. Then place the leg in the jig and align the marked point with the bit. Holding the leg with one hand, bore a countersunk hole three-quarters of the way through the stock *(above, left)*. Then outline a notch on the bottom end of each leg perpendicular to the hole, making its width equal to the thickness of the rockers and its height about one-half the rocker height. Cut the sides of the notches on your band saw, then remove the waste between the kerfs, shaving away the wood in thin layers with a chisel. Clamp a stop block in place with an arc cut out of one face to steady the workpiece *(above, right)*.

PREPARING THE ARMS AND THE ROCKERS

1 Cutting the arms and rockers
Referring to the anatomy illustration on page 38, make a template for the arms. Outline the shape on one arm blank, then flip the template over and outline the second arm; this will ensure that the two are mirror images of each other. On each arm, also mark the mortise that will accept the tenon at the top end of the front leg. Cut the arms to shape on your band saw *(right)*. Repeat the process to saw the rockers.

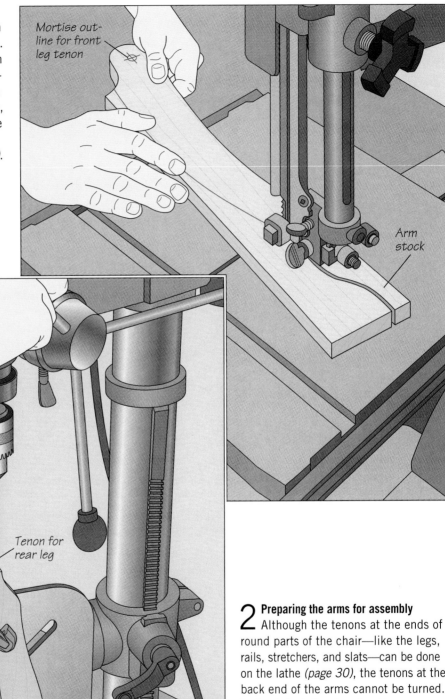

Mortise outline for front leg tenon

Arm stock

Tenon for rear leg

2 Preparing the arms for assembly
Although the tenons at the ends of round parts of the chair—like the legs, rails, stretchers, and slats—can be done on the lathe *(page 30)*, the tenons at the back end of the arms cannot be turned. Instead, install a dowel cutter on your drill press, tilt the machine table 90° and clamp the arm in place with the tenon-end centered under the cutter. Set the drilling depth at one-half the leg diameter then cut the tenon *(left)*.

ASSEMBLING THE ROCKING CHAIR

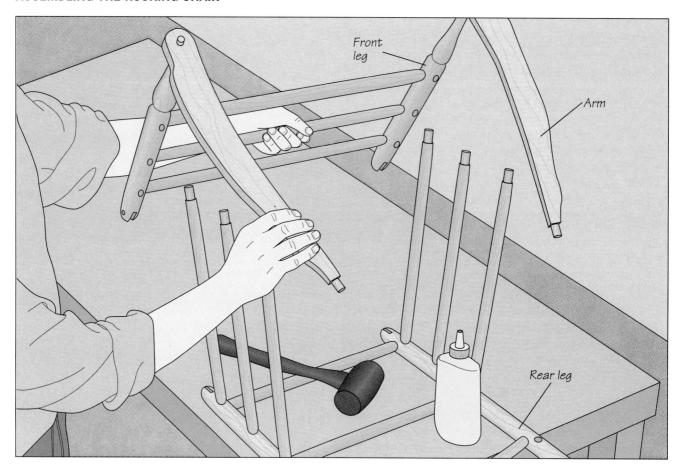

Front leg

Arm

Rear leg

1 Gluing the front and rear leg assemblies together
Gluing up the rocking chair follows much the same procedure used for the Enfield chair. Start by attaching the crest rail, slats, rails, and stretchers to the two rear legs *(page 33)*. Then glue the arms, rails, and stretchers to the front legs. Once the adhesive has cured, spread glue on the tenons of the side rails and stretchers and in their mortises in the legs and fit the two assemblies together *(above)*. Use a dead-blow hammer to tap the joints into final position.

2 Making the arm buttons
Prepare two blanks and drill a mortise halfway through each one sized to accept the tenon at the top end of the front legs. Glue a length of dowel in each hole, then use the dowel to mount one of the blanks on your lathe. Turn the button to shape, then smooth it with sandpaper while it is still spinning on the lathe *(right)*. Remove the button from the machine and drill out the dowel.

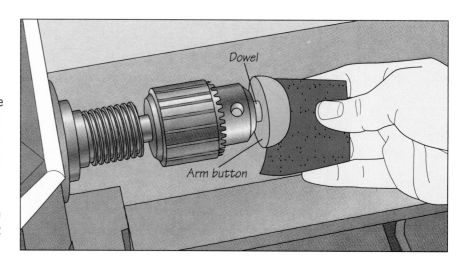

Dowel

Arm button

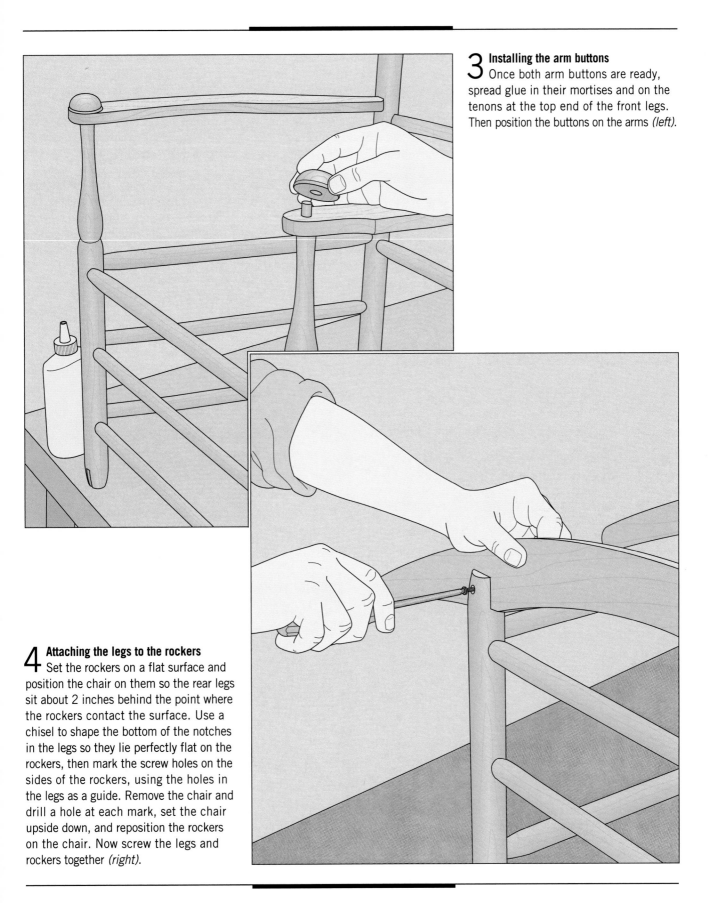

3 Installing the arm buttons
Once both arm buttons are ready, spread glue in their mortises and on the tenons at the top end of the front legs. Then position the buttons on the arms *(left)*.

4 Attaching the legs to the rockers
Set the rockers on a flat surface and position the chair on them so the rear legs sit about 2 inches behind the point where the rockers contact the surface. Use a chisel to shape the bottom of the notches in the legs so they lie perfectly flat on the rockers, then mark the screw holes on the sides of the rockers, using the holes in the legs as a guide. Remove the chair and drill a hole at each mark, set the chair upside down, and reposition the rockers on the chair. Now screw the legs and rockers together *(right)*.

TAPE SEAT

S haker tape, called listing by the Shakers, began to supplant other types of woven seat materials after 1830. Its range of colors, neat appearance, durability, and ease of installation made it ideal for furniture builders bent on producing quality goods as efficiently as possible. And unlike cane or other naturally occurring materials, tape does not dry out or split; nor does it pinch or snag clothing.

Shown below and on the following pages, weaving is fairly simple. One length of tape, called the warp, is anchored to the side rails and wrapped around the front and back seat rails in adjoining rows. A second length, called the weft, is woven alternately under and over the strands that form the warp. Loose ends are joined by weaving them back on themselves, ensuring that the rows always remain parallel.

Shaker tape is available in ⅝- and 1-inch widths from folk-art suppliers. You can weave the basic tabby style shown in this section or create a wide variety of designs that include basic and complex geometric shapes.

The Shaker rocking chair shown at left features canvas tape seating as well as a tape back.

WEAVING A TAPE SEAT

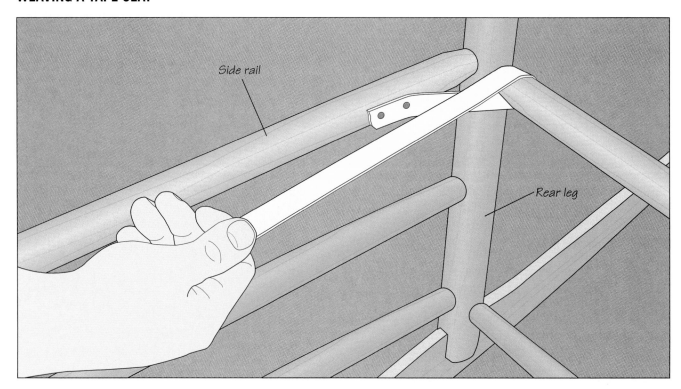

1 Anchoring the warp rows
Tack a length of tape to the inside of a side seat rail about 2 inches from the rear leg so that the tape is parallel to the rail. Loop the tape around the back rail from underneath, ensuring the edge of the material butts against the rear leg *(above)*. Wrap the tape around the front rail and pull it towards the back rail from underneath.

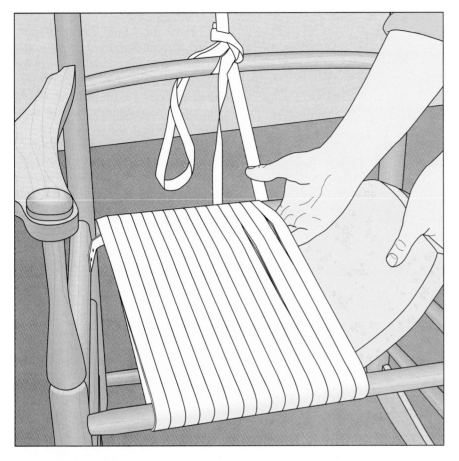

2 Stuffing the seat

Continue wrapping the warp around the front and back rails from underneath, making sure adjoining rows of tape are in contact. The weave should be tight, but not so taut that there is no play for the weft rows to be woven between the warp rows. Once you are about halfway to the opposite side rail, it is time to stuff the seat. To prevent the tape from slackening, tie the loose length of tape to one of the slats. Buy a piece of 1-inch-thick foam padding from a craft supply or hardware store and cut it with a craft knife to fit within the seat rails. Slip the padding between the tape layers *(left)*, centering it between the rails.

3 Completing the warp

Continue weaving the warp rows until you reach the opposite side rail and the back seat rail is entirely wrapped in tape. Then temporarily tack the loose length of tape to the side rail *(below)* and cut off the loose end.

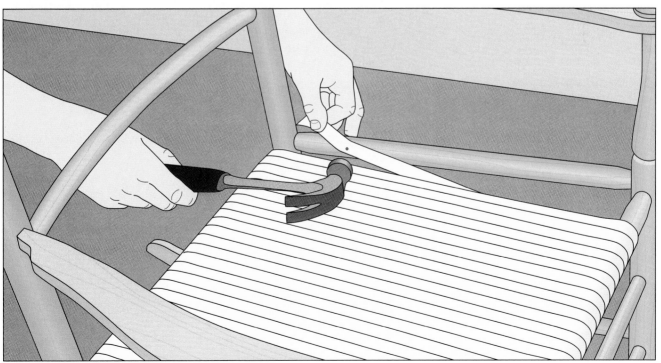

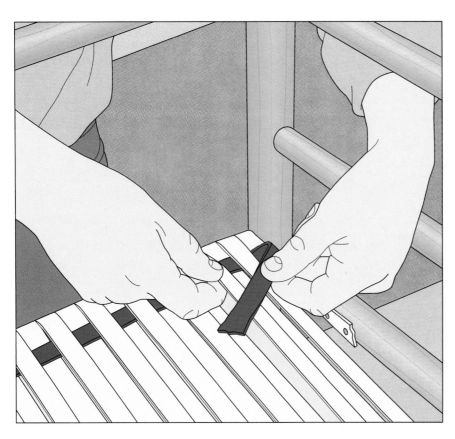

4 Starting the weft
Set the chair upside down on a work surface that will enable you to work comfortably. Starting along the back seat rail opposite the place where you began the warp, slip the end of the weft tape under the first strand of the warp, over the next, and continue with this under-and-over weave until you reach the last warp strand. Pull the excess tape through, leaving 5 inches or so at the starting point. Weave this part back on itself to anchor the tape in place *(left)*. Flip the chair upright and continue weaving on the top side of the seat.

5 Filling the gaps in the warp
Weave about three rows of weft, then begin filling in the triangular gaps left along the side rails where you installed the warp. Cut a length of warp tape long enough to weave two rows of seating, plus about 5 inches, and slip the tape under the last strand of weft beneath the seat and around the front seat rail, butting it against the last row of warp you wove in step 3. Then return to the back rail, passing the tape under the last weft row and over the second one *(right)*. Weave another warp row adjacent to the last one the same way. Leave the excess hanging for now; you will be able to weave it into the subsequent weft rows. Weave three more weft rows and repeat the gap-filling process.

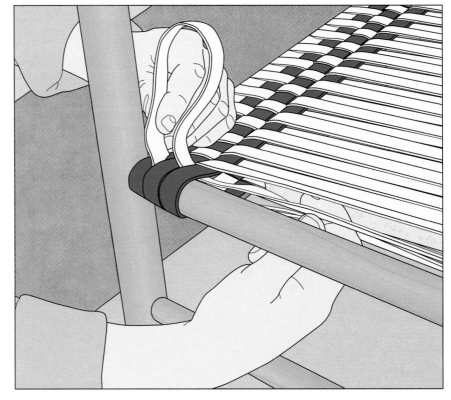

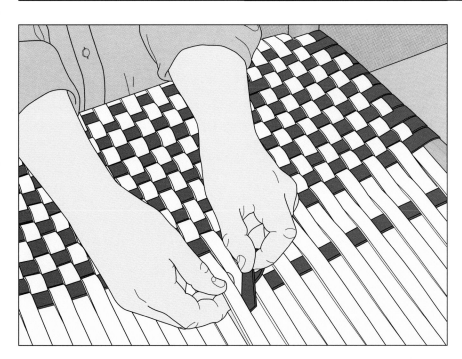

6 Completing the weft rows

Continue weaving the weft, wrapping each row around the side rails and weaving over and under the warp rows *(left)*. Avoid twisting the material. As you finish each row, pull it tight against the previous one with your fingers. As you work your way toward the side rail, the warp will become increasingly tight. To make space for the weft, slide a blunt knife between the warp rows as necessary. When you have laid down the final weft row, weave it back on itself to hold it in place. Also weave in any loose ends of tape on the underside of the seat.

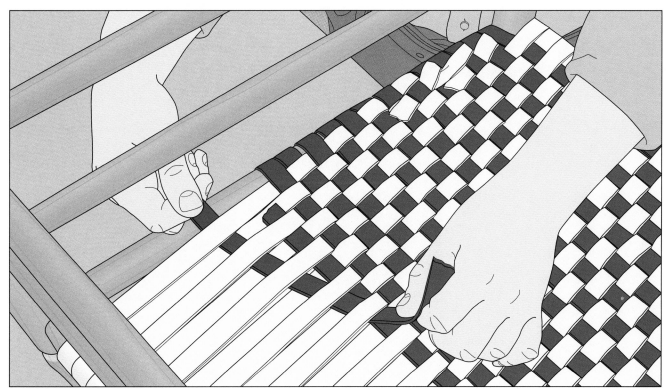

7 Splicing tape

If you run out of tape before finishing the warp or the weft, you will need to join two ends. You can stitch them together with thread, but a simpler method is to start weaving a new length at a point about 6 inches before the end of the first tape *(above)*, overlapping the tapes and binding them together by friction. Use this technique on the underside of the seat with the chair upside down so that no seams or bulges will be visible.

MEETINGHOUSE BENCH

T he meetinghouse bench served as a pew for the Shakers. During services, the faithful would sit and listen to a sermon delivered by an elder. At the close of the meeting, the benches would be moved out of the way and hung from a pegboard *(page 138)*. With the floor cleared, the Shakers' ritual dancing—

Made of cherry with a pine seat, the meetinghouse bench shown at left is modeled after those used by Shaker worshippers. Because people are larger than they were in the Shakers' time, the seat is wider than that of an original bench.

from which they derive their name— would begin.

Although many Shaker communities had benches of the style shown in this section, the design is believed to have originated in Enfield, New Hampshire. Typically, the crest rail, legs, and spindles were built from maple or cherry and the seat from pine. Many early examples remain intact, as a result of sound construction and careful handling by their makers.

As shown below, the bench's legs are raked to the front and back, but are not splayed sideways. The spindles and crest rail are tapered and the rail is angled at the ends.

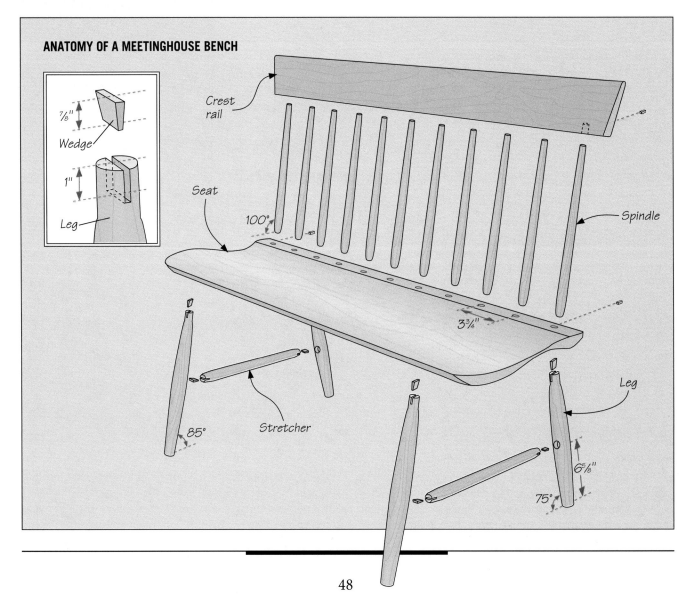

ANATOMY OF A MEETINGHOUSE BENCH

CUTTING LIST

ITEM	QTY	L	W OR DIA.	TH
Seat	1	44	14	1½
Crest rail	1	44	4	¾
Spindles*	11	14	¾	
Legs*	4	17	1½	
Stretchers*	2	14	¾	

*Note: Dimensions include tenon lengths.

PREPARING THE SEAT

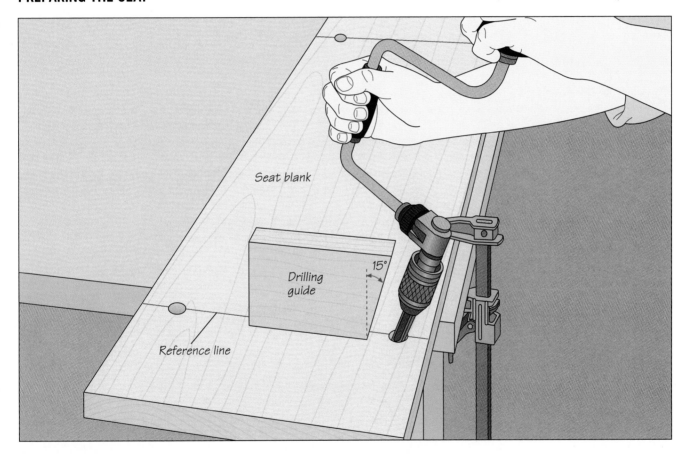

Seat blank

Drilling
guide

15°

Reference line

1 Drilling the leg holes

Clamp your seat blank bottom-face up on a work surface and mark a reference line across the surface 5 inches from each end, then pinpoint the holes for the legs; the back holes should be 1¼ inches from the back edge of the seat and the front holes should be 1¾ inches from the front edge. Fit a hand brace with a spoon bit the same diameter as the legs. To help you drill the holes at the correct rake angle, make two guides from a short wood scrap, mitering the guide for the front legs at 5° and the one for the back legs at 15°. Set the appropriate guide on edge on the reference line a few inches from the hole mark and hold the bit parallel to the mitered edge of the guide. Then bore the hole *(above)*, stopping when you are about two-thirds of the way through the stock—about 1 inch deep.

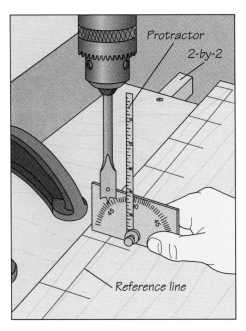

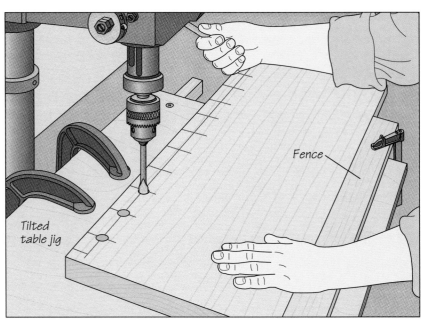

2 Drilling the spindle holes

Bore the holes for the seat spindles using your drill press and a shop-made jig. Mark a reference line on the top face of the seat parallel to the back edge and 1 inch away from it. Then mark the spindle holes, starting about 2½ inches from the ends and spacing the remaining holes equally. To ensure that the spindles are tilted back at the correct angle, adjust a protractor to 10° and use the shop-made tilted table jig shown above to tilt the seat in relation to the bit. For the jig, set a piece of plywood on the machine table, place the seat blank on top, and slip a 2-by-2 under the plywood parallel with its back edge. Holding the protractor base on the seat and the blade next to the bit, reposition the 2-by-2 until the blade is parallel to the bit *(above, left)*. Then screw the 2-by-2 to the plywood and clamp the jig to the machine table. To drill the holes, set the drilling depth at two-thirds the seat thickness, align the first mark under the bit, and clamp a board to the jig as a fence along the seat front's edge. Then, holding the seat against the fence, bore each hole *(above, right)*.

3 Preparing to shape the seat's top

Cut the recess on the seat's top surface on your table saw. Start by marking the profile of the seat on the workpiece. Referring to the anatomy illustration on page 48, outline the shape of the ends on the bottom face and end grain of the blank. To outline the recess, set the seat top face-down on your table saw and crank the blade to the desired depth of cut. Position the seat so the recess will be centered between the middle and the back edge, then outline the blade on the end of the stock and mark a reference line on the saw table along the seat's front edge *(right)*. Now clamp a board as a guide so that its edge is aligned with the reference line.

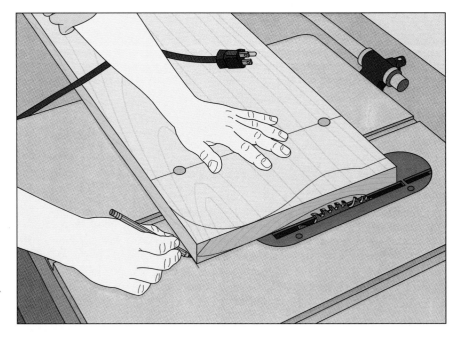

Guide board

4 Cutting the recess in the seat top
Adjust the blade to a cutting height of
$\frac{1}{16}$ inch. Slowly feed the seat across the
table with one hand, while pressing it
against the guide board with the other.
Make as many passes as necessary until
the blade outline on the end of the stock
disappears *(left)*, raising the blade $\frac{1}{16}$ inch
at a time. For a smooth finish, raise the
blade very slightly and make a final pass.

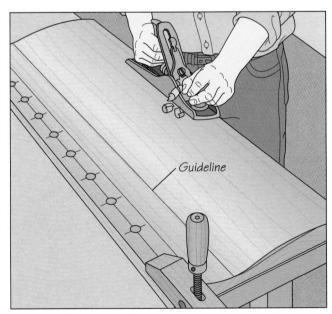

Guideline

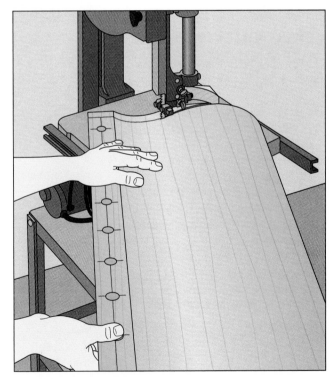

5 Shaping the top of the seat
Clamp the seat face-up on a work surface and mark a
guideline along the length of the recess you cut as a reminder
of where the curved portion of the seat top will end. Referring
to the outline on the end of the stock, use a hand plane to finish shaping the seat top *(above)*, removing waste from end to
end and always cutting with the grain. Continue until you
reach your outline.

6 Cutting the ends of the seat
Following the cutting lines on the top face of the seat, cut
the ends on your band saw *(above)*. Keep the workpiece flat on
the machine table as you feed it, then sand the cut ends smooth.

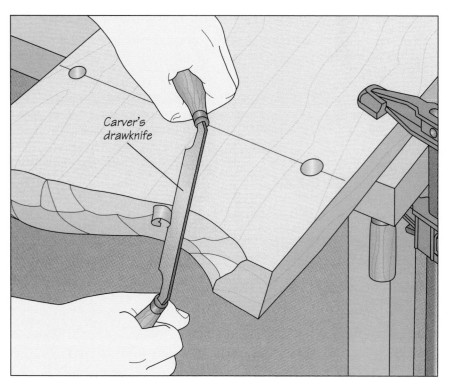

Carver's drawknife

7 Shaping the underside of the seat
The ends and front edge of the seat are beveled on its underside. Bevel the front edge of the seat on your table saw, tilting the blade to a 45° angle. The ends are best shaped by hand with a carver's drawknife. Clamp the seat face-down on a work surface. Then, holding the tool in both hands with the blade bevel-down at a 45° angle to the end of the seat, pull it toward you to shave off waste wood *(left)*. Once you are satisfied with the bevel, sand the ends smooth.

JOINING THE LEGS TO THE SEAT

1 Preparing the legs for the stretchers
Turn the legs on your lathe *(page 28)*, tapering them to a diameter of ¾ inch at the top and ¹⁵⁄₁₆ inch at the bottom. Also turn the stretchers into cylinders, forming a tenon *(page 29)* at each end. To ensure that the stretcher holes in the legs will be at the correct angle, drill them with the seat face-down on a work surface and the legs dry-fitted in their holes in the seat. Install a spade bit in an electric drill and wrap a strip of masking tape around the bit to mark the drilling depth—about one-half the diameter of the leg. Also mark a point halfway up each leg (see the anatomy on page 48). Then holding the leg in its hole and the bit parallel to the seat surface, drill the hole at the mark, stopping when the masking tape contacts the stock *(right)*.

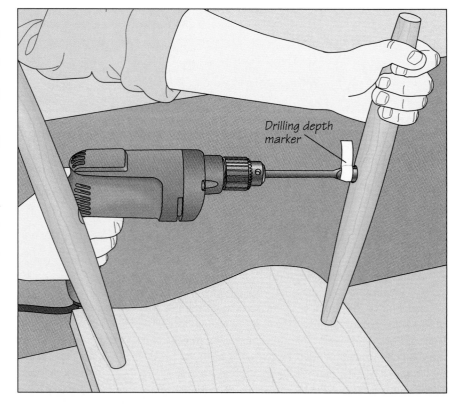

Drilling depth marker

2 Preparing the legs and stretchers for wedges

Reinforce the joints connecting the legs to the seat and the stretchers to the legs with wedges. Cut the kerfs for the wedges on your band saw. When you are kerfing the legs, hold the leg on the machine table with the stretcher hole facing straight up. This will ensure that the wedges in the legs are perpendicular to the grain of the seat, preventing the seat from splitting. Feed the workpiece into the blade, slicing a kerf to a depth of about ½ inch *(right)*. Cut the kerfs in the stretchers the same way, making sure that the wedges will be perpendicular to the grain of the legs.

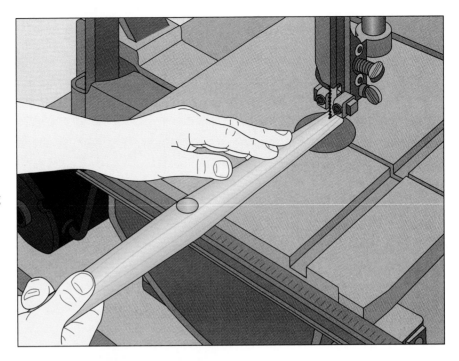

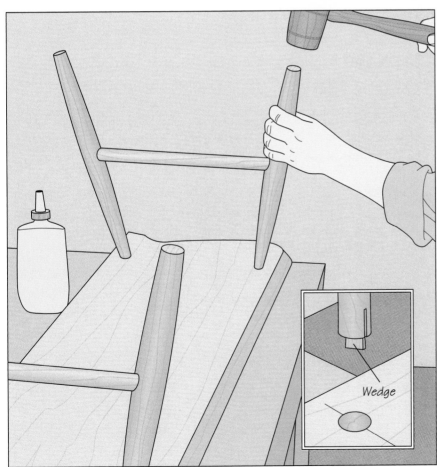

Wedge

3 Gluing up the legs and stretchers

To make wedges for the kerfs, cut some hardwood pieces on the band saw slightly less than ½ inch long and ⅛ inch thick at the base, tapering to a point. Start by gluing the stretchers to the legs. Spread some adhesive on the wedges and in the kerfs as well as on the stretcher tenons and the mortises in the legs, and insert the wedges into their kerfs. Fit the stretcher and legs together, using a wooden mallet to tap the pieces into final position. You can leave the wedges protruding from the kerfs *(inset)*; they will sit flush with the ends of the legs and stretchers when you tap the joints together. Next, glue the wedges into the legs, spread adhesive on the contacting surfaces between the legs and the seat, and tap the legs into position *(left)*.

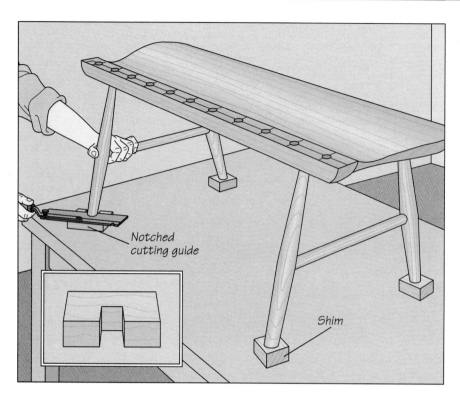

4 Sawing the legs to length
The technique shown above will ensure that all four legs are precisely the same length. Cut four wood blocks from a single board, then notch one of the blocks to fit around a leg *(inset)*. Place the block around the first leg to be cut. Holding the leg firmly with one hand, cut it to size with a flush-cutting saw. Once the first leg is trimmed, remove the notched block and replace it with one of the remaining blocks. Position the notched piece around the next leg and make the cut. Continue in this way until all four legs are cut *(right)*. If you want the bench to have a backward slant, tack shims to the bottoms of the front legs before trimming the legs.

Notched cutting guide

Shim

GLUING THE CREST RAIL AND SPINDLES TO THE SEAT

1 Preparing the crest rail for the spindles
Cut the crest rail to size, then mark the spindle holes on its bottom edge, using the holes you drilled in the seat as a guide. Clamp a piece of plywood as an auxiliary table to your drill press, install a brad-point bit, and adjust the drilling depth to about 1 inch. Align the first hole mark under the bit and clamp a board to the auxiliary table flush against the face of the rail. This will serve as a fence to position the rail. Butting the rail against the fence, drill the holes *(right)*.

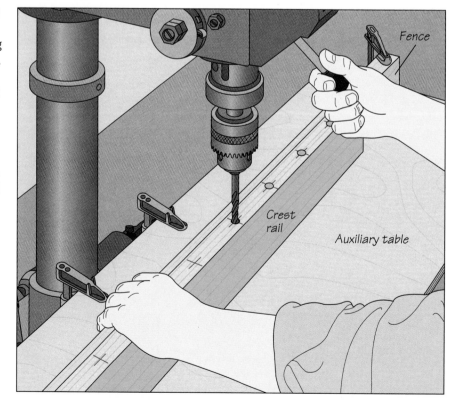

Fence

Crest rail

Auxiliary table

2 Gluing up the spindles and crest rail

Set the seat face-up on a work surface, then spread glue on the ends of the spindles and in the holes in the seat and the crest rail. Fit the spindles into the seat, tapping each one into final position with a dead-blow hammer *(above)*. Once all the spindles are in place, fit the rail on top and tap it into position. For additional reinforcement, you can peg the joints between the spindle and the seat and rail at each end of the bench. Drill the peg holes into the spindles through the back edge of the seat and the outside face of the rail, following the procedure explained on page 110.

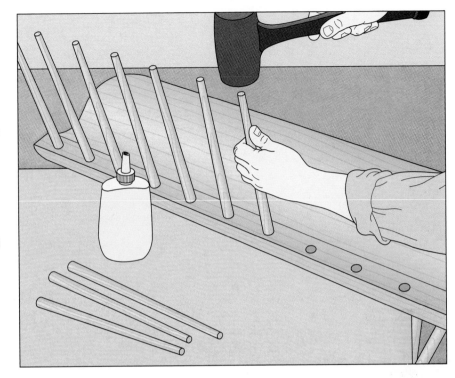

SHOP TIP

Tapering the crest rail on a planer
If you wish to taper the crest rail of the bench so the top edge is narrower than the bottom, use a thickness planer and a shop-made jig. For the jig, tack two wood strips to a board that is longer and wider than the rail. One of the strips should be twice as thick as the other, and the gap between them should be about 1 inch less than the width of the rail. Clamp the jig to the planer table so the board and the strips extend from each side of the machine by several inches. Now turn on the planer and make a pass through the machine with the bottom edge of the rail flush against the thicker strip and the top edge propped up on the thinner strip. Make as many passes as necessary to achieve the desired taper. Then turn the rail over and repeat the process, this time with the rail's bottom edge butted against the thinner strip, as shown above.

TABLES

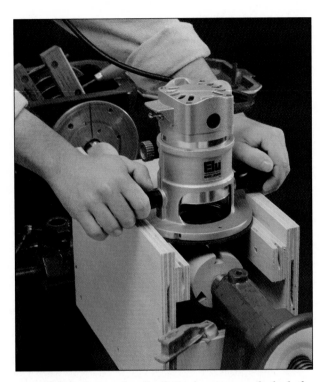

With help from a shop-built jig that rests on the bed of a lathe, a router fitted with a dovetail bit plows sockets in the column of a candle stand. The sockets will mate with sliding dovetails at the top ends of the legs. For instructions on making this jig, refer to page 81.

The early years of Shaker communities were far from bountiful. As one resident of the Hancock village said in 1791, "Our food was very scanty. But what we had, we ate with thankful hearts. For breakfast and supper, we lived mostly upon bean porridge and water porridge." By the second decade of the 19th Century, however, the Shakers' capacity for ceaseless hard work began to pay off in material prosperity.

Shaker dining tables are mute testament to the communities' success in fields, barns, and gardens. As increasing numbers of converts joined the movement, mealtimes saw the Shakers crowded elbow to elbow around the dinner table, eating in solemn silence and, as in most of their other activities, with the men and women separated.

Trestle tables *(page 58)* were common fixtures in most Shaker dining halls. With their narrow legs and unobstructed legroom allowing people to sit quite close together, the tables were well suited to the Shaker ethic. To facilitate the passing of food across the large tops, settings were divided into "squares" of four diners. Typically 10 feet long, Shaker trestle tables were built to seat three squares of 12 people. The 6-foot-long table illustrated on page 58 seats eight comfortably.

Drop-leaf tables *(page 68)*, with their expandable tops, were developed later than trestle types, becoming common by 1820. They were used in the dining hall as side tables or, occasionally, as dining tables. But the drop-leaf design is so practical that the Shakers found a multitude of applications for it everywhere from the dairy to the infirmary.

The pedestal table *(page 78)*, or candle stand, was very popular with the Shakers. Strong and sturdy, it was light enough to move easily. Its tripod legs kept it from wobbling. The Shakers experimented endlessly with this basic form. The stand was built with convex, concave, or turned legs. Tops were made round, square or rectangular. Sometimes, the tops were simply rounded over or lipped, and some featured underslung drawers to hold sewing supplies. Some tops had a groove in the lip to help in the packaging of seeds. (Oval or octagonal shapes were excluded, however, as being frivolous and too worldly.) The candle stand shown in this chapter is but one version of a popular and functional design.

A wooden support is pivoted under the leaf of the drop-leaf table shown at left. Over time, the support may tend to sag slightly, but the thin wedge glued to the underside of the leaf will compensate for the change, allowing the leaf to sit at the same level as the top.

TRESTLE TABLE

Despite their large size, trestle tables are easy to move. This is because the joints connecting the feet to the legs, the legs to the rails, and the rails to the top are fixed not by glue, but by screws and bolts. The table shown below relies heavily on knockdown hardware, a modern version of the Shaker practice of assembling tables with bolts that drew against a trapped nut, allowing easy disassembly. Shakers frequently used cherry for their tables; this remains a good choice today.

To prevent the top from warping and also to hide end grain, a tongue is cut along each end to position the mating groove of a breadboard end. The ends are screwed to the top, with only a little glue applied at the middle. This allows the top to expand and contract across its width as humidity changes without being hindered by the breadboard ends.

As shown on page 59, the first step in making this table is gluing up the top. Because of its width, the top cannot be passed through most thickness planers after glue up. Instead, start by assembling the top in the largest possible sections that your machine can handle and plane them to a uniform thickness. Then glue the sections together, being very careful to ensure that they are perfectly flush.

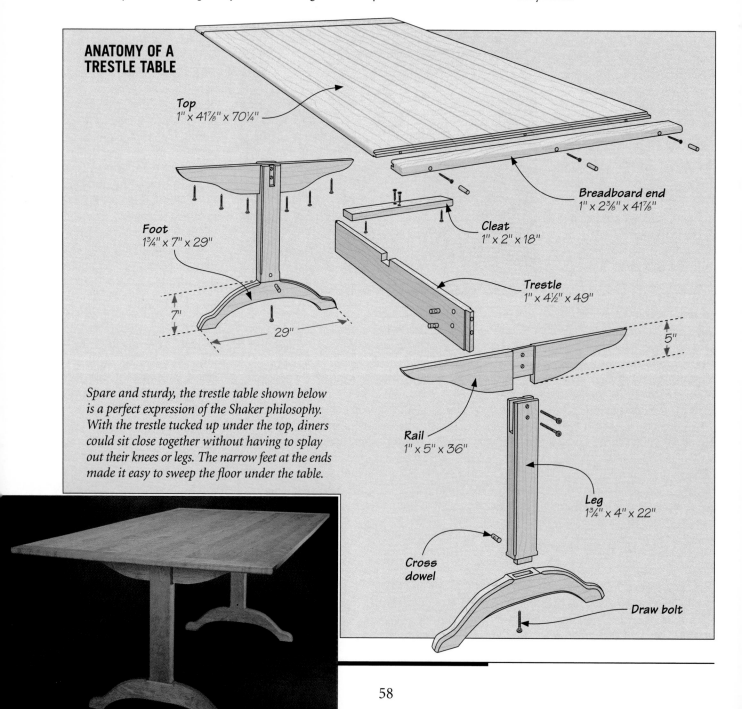

ANATOMY OF A TRESTLE TABLE

Top
1" x 41⅞" x 70¼"

Foot
1¾" x 7" x 29"

7"

29"

Breadboard end
1" x 2⅜" x 41⅞"

Cleat
1" x 2" x 18"

Trestle
1" x 4½" x 49"

5"

Rail
1" x 5" x 36"

Leg
1¾" x 4" x 22"

Cross dowel

Draw bolt

Spare and sturdy, the trestle table shown below is a perfect expression of the Shaker philosophy. With the trestle tucked up under the top, diners could sit close together without having to splay out their knees or legs. The narrow feet at the ends made it easy to sweep the floor under the table.

MAKING THE TOP

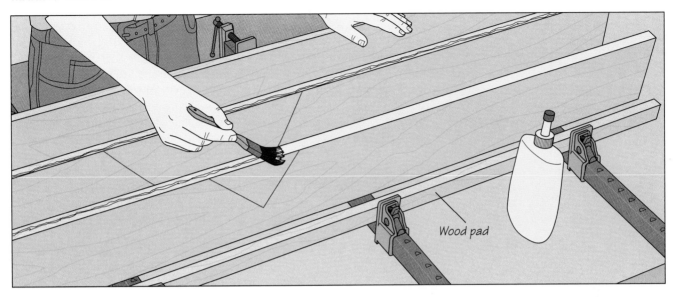

Wood pad

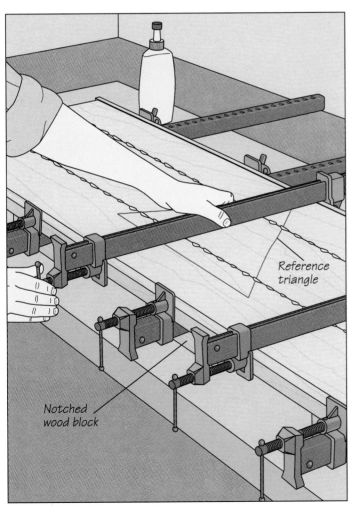

Reference triangle

Notched wood block

1 Applying the glue

Once all your boards are jointed and ripped to a combined width that is roughly 1 inch wider than the finished top, arrange the boards for the best possible match of color, figure, and grain. To minimize warping, lay out the planks so that the end grain of adjacent boards runs in opposite directions, then mark a reference triangle on top of the boards. This will help you correctly realign them for glue up. To hold your bar clamps upright, cut notched wood blocks and set the clamps in the blocks. Space the clamps every 24 to 36 inches. To protect the stock, also cut two wood pads as long and as thick as the planks. Apply a narrow bead of glue to one edge of each joint and use a small, stiff-bristled brush to spread the adhesive evenly on the board edges *(above)*.

2 Tightening clamps

Lay the boards face up on the bar clamps and align their ends, making sure the sides of the reference triangle are lined up. Tighten the clamps under the boards just enough to butt them together. To balance the clamping pressure and keep the panel flat, place bar clamps across the top of the panel between the ones underneath. As you tighten the clamps, make sure that the boards are perfectly flush. Place a scrap of wood on any high spots where two boards meet and hit it with a hammer until the two lie flat. Finish tightening all the clamps in turn *(left)* until there are no gaps between the boards and a thin, even bead of glue squeezes out of the joints. Once all the top sections are glued up, plane them and glue them together.

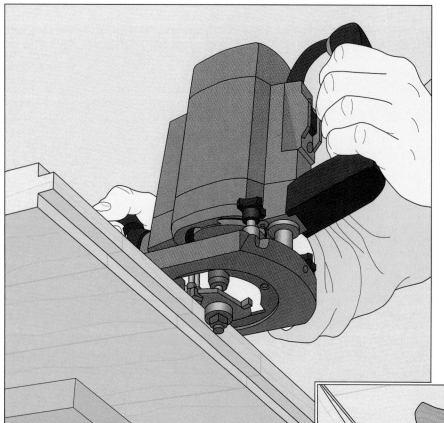

3 Preparing the top for the breadboard ends

The breadboard ends are attached to the top with a tongue-and-groove joint. Start by routing a tongue at each end of the top. Install a piloted three-wing slotting cutter in a router and set the cutting depth to ¼-inch; this will enable you to clear the waste from each side of the tongue in two passes. Secure the top to a work surface and turn the router on with the bit clear of the stock. Make the first pass on both sides of each end making sure the bit's pilot bearing is butted against the end of the top. Then reset the depth of cut slightly deeper to rout the rest of the waste from half of the tongue; the tongue should be one-third the thickness of the top. Finish the tongues at both ends *(left)*.

4 Making and installing the breadboard ends

Plane the breadboard ends to the same thickness as the top, then saw them as long as the top's width. Cut the grooves along the inside edges of the breadboard ends on your table saw *(page 62)*. The grooves should be as wide as the tongues you routed in step 3 and slightly deeper than their length. Fit the ends in position and counterbore three holes through each one and into the top, locating one hole at the middle and another a few inches from each end. Use a file to elongate the holes in the breadboard ends slightly; this will facilitate wood movement. Spread glue on the tongues about 1 inch to each side of the center, then reposition the breadboard ends *(right)*, using a mallet and a wood block, if necessary, to tap them into final position. Drive the screws to secure the ends, glue wood plugs over the heads, and trim them flush with a chisel. Sand the surface smooth.

Breadboard end

MAKING THE FEET

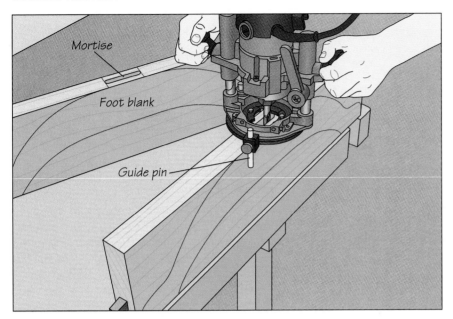

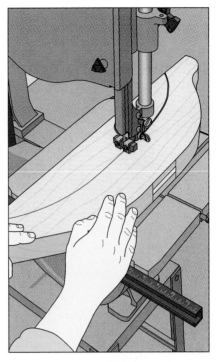

1 Preparing the feet for the legs

Outline the feet on blanks and cut the mortises in them with a router and the commercial mortising jig shown above. The jig features two guide pins that butt against opposite faces of a workpiece, ensuring that the mortise is centered on the edge. Install a ½-inch mortising bit in a router and set the cutting depth to cut the 1⅛-inch-deep mortise in three or four passes. Secure one foot edge up on your bench and mark the beginning and end of the mortise. Plunge the bit into the stock at one end of the mortise, then feed the cutter to the other end, making sure the guide pins both ride along the workpiece throughout the cut. Repeat for the other foot, then square the corners of the mortises with a chisel.

2 Sawing the feet to shape

Cut the leg on your band saw, sawing the top edge first, followed by the bottom edge (above). Sand the cut edges smooth.

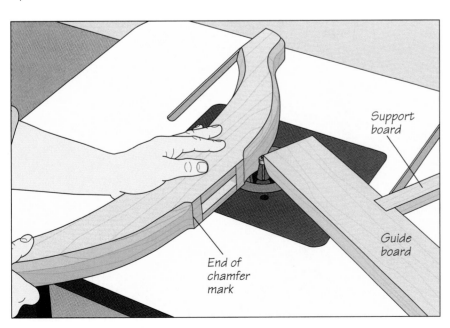

3 Chamfering the top edges of the feet

Install a piloted 45-degree bit in a router, mount the tool in a table and set the cutting depth for a ½-inch-wide chamfer. To prevent kickback, clamp a notched guide board to the table so its edge is in line with the bit's pilot bearing. Reinforce the guide with a support board. To indicate where the chamfer ends, mark a line across the top edge of the foot ¾ inch from each end of the mortise. Feed the foot into the cutter, riding the stock along the guide board to start the pass, then pivot the workpiece away from the guide, making sure the stock butts against the bearing. Stop the cut at the chamfer line. Repeat on the other side of the mortise, then turn the foot over and chamfer the opposite face (left).

MAKING THE LEGS AND RAILS

1 Sawing the tenons at the bottom of the legs

Cut the legs to size, then outline the tenons on their bottom ends, using the mortises in the feet as a guide. Cut the tenons on your table saw fitted with a dado head; adjust the width of the head to slightly more than one-half the tenon length—about 1 inch. You will saw the tenon sides and edges in two passes each, eliminating the need to attach an auxiliary fence. To position the rip fence, align the shoulder line on the leg with the dado head and butt the fence against the end of the board; the fence should be well clear of the blades. Start by cutting the sides of the tenon *(page 71)*. For the edges, align the end of the board with the dado head and make a pass, then turn the leg over and repeat. To complete the tenon, align the shoulder line with the head and feed the board with the miter gauge, riding the end of the workpiece against the fence. Turn the board over and repeat *(left)*.

2 Preparing the legs for the trestle

The trestle fits into a stopped groove at the top of the leg. Adjust the width of the dado head and the cutting height to ⅝ inch. Center the face of the leg over the dado head and butt the fence against the edge. Mark the end of the groove on the legs and the points on the table insert where the blades stop cutting; this will help you determine the position of the dado head when it is hidden by the workpiece during the cut. To saw the groove, feed the leg face down, holding the edge against the fence *(right)*. Once the cutting line on the leg aligns with the mark on the table insert, lift the workpiece off the dado head. Square the stopped end of the dado with a chisel. You can now cut a two-shouldered tenon at each end of the stretcher *(page 71)* to fit into the groove.

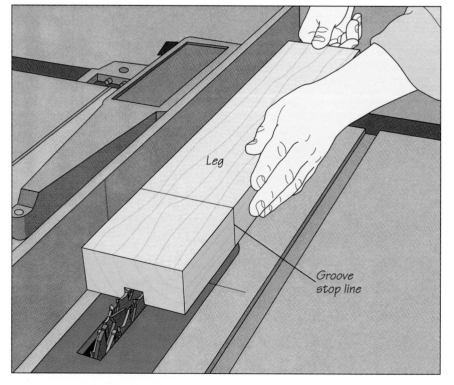

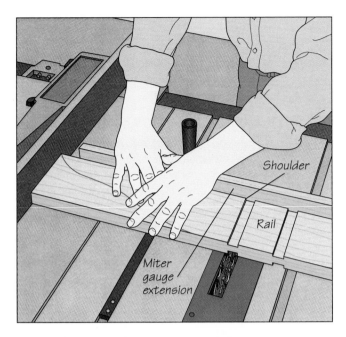

Shoulder

Rail

Miter
gauge
extension

3 Preparing the rails for the legs

The rails are attached to the top ends of the legs with bridle joints. Start by cutting the recesses in the rails that enable them to mesh with the mortises you will saw in the legs. Outline the rail profile on your blanks and mark the shoulders of the recesses 2 inches to each side of the middle of the boards. Adjust the dado head on your table saw as wide as it will go and set the cutting height at ¼ inch. Screw an extension to the miter gauge, align one of the shoulder marks on the rail with the dado head, and butt the fence against the end of the stock. Feed the rail with the miter gauge, pressing the stock against the fence. Flip the rail to cut a shoulder on the other face, then rotate the piece and cut the shoulders at the other end of the recesses *(left)*. Move the fence out of the way and remove the remaining waste.

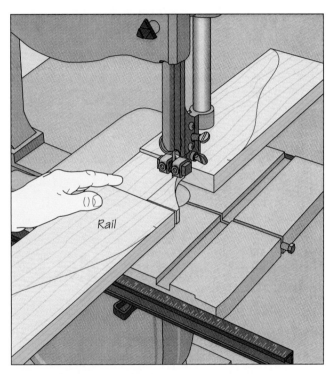

Rail

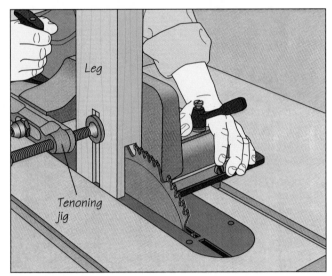

Leg

Tenoning
jig

4 Sawing the mortises in the legs

Replace the dado head on your table saw with a combination blade, crank it as high as it will go, and cut the mortises at the top ends of the legs with the help of a commercial tenoning jig; the model shown above slides in the miter slot. Clamp the leg upright in the jig, position the jig to center the blade on the edge of the workpiece, and feed the stock into the cut. Then move the jig very slightly away from the blade to enlarge the mortise. Make another pass, turn the leg around in the jig, and feed it into the blade again *(above)*. Next, test-fit one of the rails in the mortise. If the fit is too tight, adjust the jig to shave a little more wood from the mortise and make two more passes, continuing until the rail fits snugly in the mortise.

5 Cutting the rails to shape

To bring the top edge of the rails flush with the top end of the legs, you will have to notch the bottom edge of the recessed section of the rails (see the anatomy on page 58). Fit the rail upside down in the leg mortise and draw a pencil along the top of the leg to mark a cutting line across the rail. Cut the notch on your band saw, starting with straight cuts along the shoulders of the recess to the marked line. Remove the remaining waste by making a curved cut from the edge to one shoulder *(above)*, then rotate the board 180° and saw along the cutting line. Once the notches in both rails are ready, saw the rails to shape as you did the feet *(page 61)* and sand the surfaces smooth.

ASSEMBLING THE TABLE

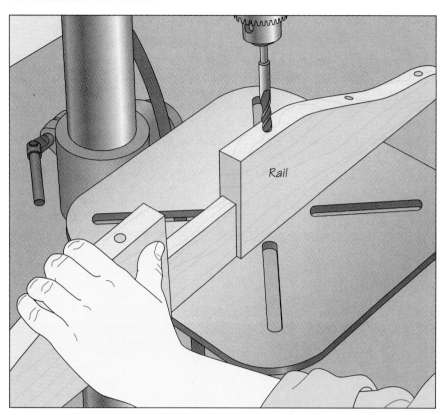

1 Preparing the rails for the top
To allow the tabletop to move, the rails are fastened to it with screws rather than glue. Mark six screw holes along the top edges of the rails—three on each side of the recesses—and bore them on your drill press. Holding the rail upright on the machine table, drill a counterbored hole through the workpiece at each mark; use curved backup boards to help you steady the rail. Then turn the rail over and enlarge the bottom of each hole *(left)*, using a ½-inch diameter bit. This will facilitate wood movement. Do not drill too deep, however; for proper anchoring, a screw requires at least 1 inch of wood with a hole no larger than its shank.

2 Preparing the feet for the legs
Using two different bits on your drill press, bore a hole through each foot for the bolt that will attach it to the leg. The bolt will be threaded into a cross dowel to provide long-grain support *(step 4)*. Start by drilling a hole to conceal a bolt head with a 1¾-inch spade bit. Mark a line on the face of the foot 1¾ inches from the bottom edge to indicate the drilling depth. Holding the foot upside down on the machine table, use the line as a guide for setting the drilling depth, then bore the bolt-recessing hole *(right)*. Then switch bits and bore a ⅜-inch-diameter clearance hole for the bolt through the foot.

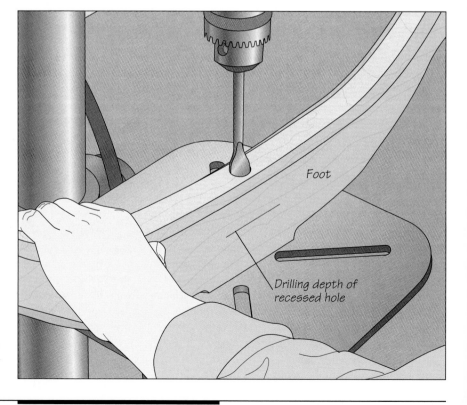

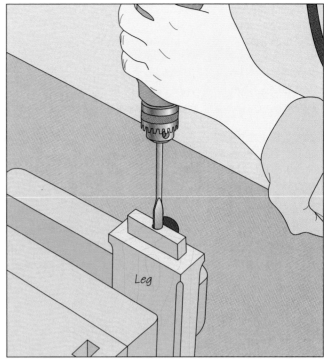

3 Drilling clearance holes in the legs

Use an electric drill to prepare the legs for the bolts from the feet. Start by fitting a foot and leg together and secure the assembly upside down in your bench vise. Insert a pencil into the hole in the foot and mark its center on the tenon at the end of the leg *(above, left)*. Then remove the foot and use the drill fitted with a ⅜-inch spade bit to bore into the tenon and leg to a depth of about 3 inches. Keep the tool perpendicular to the end of the tenon throughout the operation *(above, right)*.

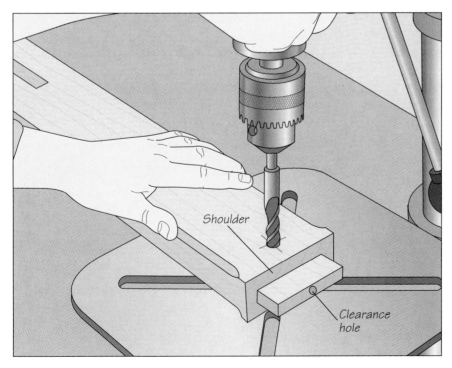

Shoulder

Clearance hole

4 Boring clearance holes in the legs for cross dowels

Install a ⁷⁄₁₆-inch brad-point bit in your drill press and set the leg inside-face up on the machine table. Adjust the drilling depth to slightly less than the stock thickness. To locate the hole for the cross dowel, mark a vertical line along the leg aligned with the pilot hole and a horizontal line across the leg ¾ inch from the shoulder of the tenon. Holding the leg steady, drill the hole *(left)*.

5 Bolting the feet to the legs

Now you are ready to assemble the table, starting with the feet and legs. Fit the pieces together and set the assembly on a work surface. Slip the cross dowel into its hole in the leg and insert the bolt up the foot. To align the fasteners so the bolt engages with the dowel, hold the dowel in position with a screwdriver as you drive the bolt with a hex driver or wrench *(right)*. Once the bolt catches in the dowel, tighten it firmly.

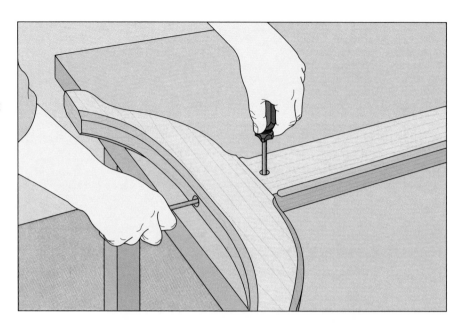

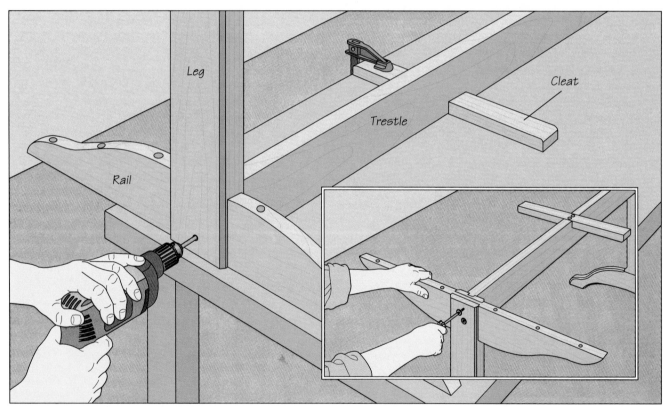

6 Assembling the legs, rails and trestle

Notch the trestle for the cleat, then screw the cleat in place. Clamp the cleat to a work surface, fit the legs and rails together, and position the legs against the trestle. The legs and rails are joined to the trestle with bolts and cross dowels. To make the connections, drill two pilot holes for bolts through each leg and rail into the end of the trestle *(above)*. Locate the holes so they pass through the rail, rather than below it, in the notched portion of the stock. Next, bore two holes near each end of the trestle for cross dowels as you did in the leg *(page 65)*, then bolt the legs and rails to the trestle *(inset)*.

7 Preparing the top

Before fastening the top to the rails, round over its top and bottom edges and ends. Lay the top face up on a work surface and start by rounding the corners slightly with a sanding block. Then install a piloted ¼-inch round-over bit in a router and set the depth of cut to shape the top's edges in two passes. Press the bit's pilot bearing against the stock as you feed the router counterclockwise along the edges and ends of the top *(right)*. Turn the top over and repeat the process with a ½-inch round-over bit to shape the bottom edges and ends.

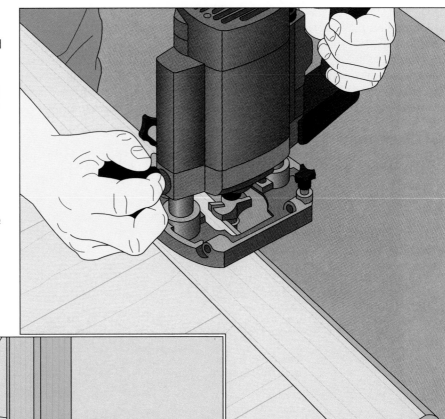

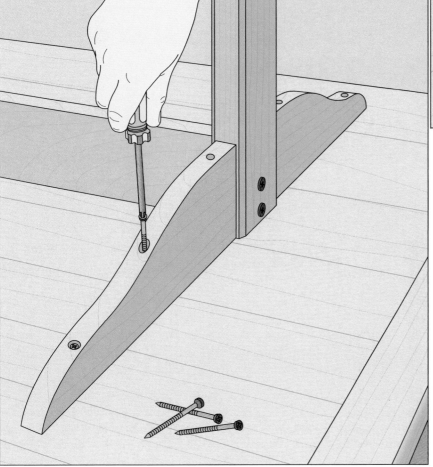

8 Attaching the top to the rails

Leave the top face down on the work surface and position the rail-and-leg assembly on it. Use an awl to mark the screw holes through the rails on the underside of the top, then drill a pilot hole for a screw at each point. Make sure the bit does not penetrate the top's upper surface. Reposition the rails on the top and screw them in place *(left)*.

DROP-LEAF TABLE

The Shakers appreciated the versatility of drop-leaf tables. The leaves could be raised when a wider top was needed, and folded down afterward so the table would occupy less space. Shaker drop-leaf tables ranged from 10-foot-long dining tables, sometimes referred to as "harvest tables," to small work tables just 2 feet long. At 41 inches long, the table shown in the illustration below is a comfortable compromise. The top can expand to a width of more than 3 feet, seating four people comfortably. With the leaves folded down, the table is less than 20 inches wide. As with most drop-leaf tables, the version shown here uses rule joints to attach the top to the leaves. To ensure adequate support for the leaves, use the largest drop-leaf hinges available, which are typically 1½ by 2⅞ inches.

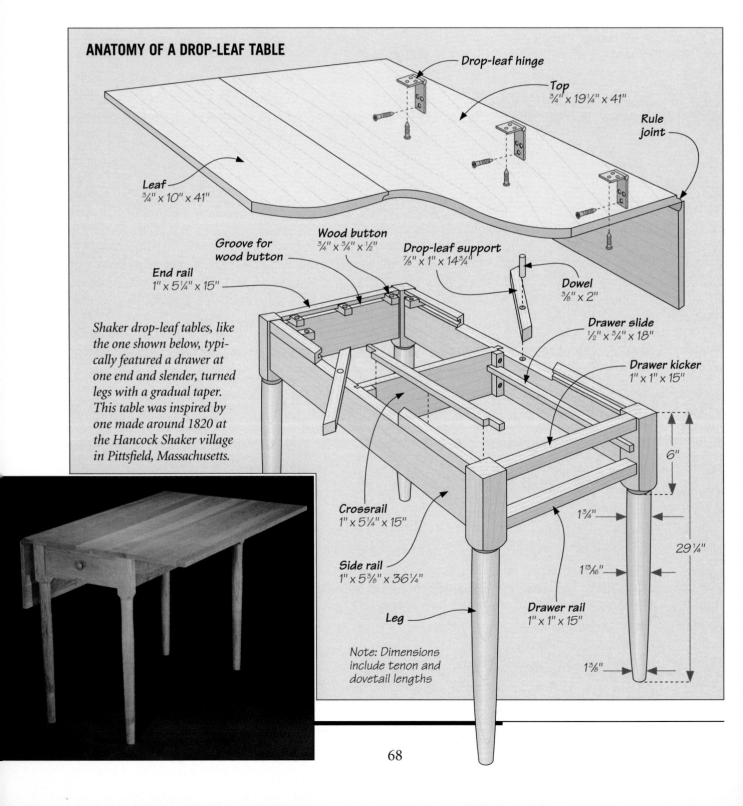

ANATOMY OF A DROP-LEAF TABLE

Drop-leaf hinge

Top
¾" x 19¼" x 41"

Rule joint

Leaf
¾" x 10" x 41"

Groove for wood button

Wood button
¾" x ¾" x ½"

Drop-leaf support
⅞" x 1" x 14¾"

Dowel
⅜" x 2"

End rail
1" x 5¼" x 15"

Drawer slide
½" x ¾" x 18"

Drawer kicker
1" x 1" x 15"

Shaker drop-leaf tables, like the one shown below, typically featured a drawer at one end and slender, turned legs with a gradual taper. This table was inspired by one made around 1820 at the Hancock Shaker village in Pittsfield, Massachusetts.

Crossrail
1" x 5¼" x 15"

Side rail
1" x 5⅜" x 36¼"

Leg

6"

1¾"

29¼"

1¹³⁄₁₆"

Drawer rail
1" x 1" x 15"

1⅜"

Note: Dimensions include tenon and dovetail lengths

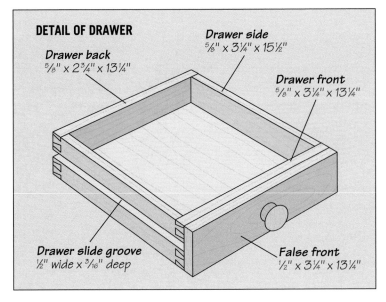

DETAIL OF DRAWER

Drawer back
5/8" x 2¾" x 13¼"

Drawer side
5/8" x 3¼" x 15½"

Drawer front
5/8" x 3¼" x 13¼"

Drawer slide groove
½" wide x ³⁄₁₆" deep

False front
½" x 3¼" x 13¼"

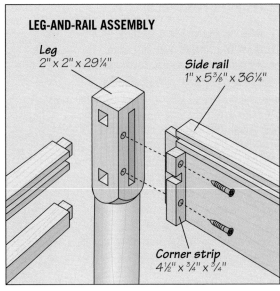

LEG-AND-RAIL ASSEMBLY

Leg
2" x 2" x 29¼"

Side rail
1" x 5⅜" x 36¼"

Corner strip
4½" x ¾" x ¾"

MAKING THE LEGS

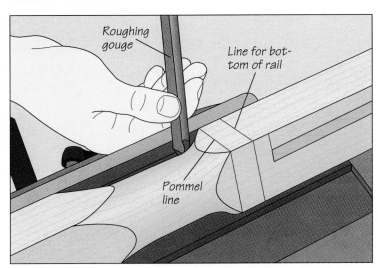

Roughing gouge

Line for bottom of rail

Pommel line

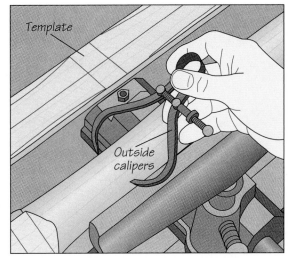

Template

Outside calipers

Cutting the mortises and turning the legs

Referring to the anatomy illustration, cut the four legs to size, then chop mortises by hand, as shown on page 91, or use a drill press equipped with a mortising bit. The mortises should be ⅜ inch wide and ⅞ inch deep, leaving space for a ½ inch shoulder on the tenon at each end. Next, turn the legs to the required shape. To help you produce four identical legs, make a hardboard template of the taper. The template should indicate the finished diameter of the legs at several different points along their lengths. Start by separating the pommel, or square section, from the cylindrical section. Mark the pommel line on the leg blanks, then mount one of them on your lathe. Define the pommel with a roughing gouge. Cut a notch at the marked line, then round the corners of the blank below the pommel. With the tip of the gouge tilted up, gradually raise the handle until the bevel is rubbing against the stock and the cutting edge is slicing into the wood *(above, left)*. Work from below the pommel toward the bottom of the leg, continuing until the blank is cylindrical and smooth. Form the taper with a spindle gouge, adjusting a separate set of calipers for each of the dimensions as marked on your template. Then check the diameter of the blank at the appropriate points *(above, right)*. Deepen the cuts if necessary until the measurements on the template and the diameter of the cuts are equal. Repeat for the remaining blanks.

PREPARING THE RAILS

1 Making the drop-leaf supports

The drop leaves are supported by pivoting supports. Housed along the top edge of the side rails, the supports pivot on dowels to hold the drop leaves when they are extended, then align with the rails when the leaves are not needed. Rip a ⅞-inch-wide strip from the edge of each side rail, then adjust your table saw's miter gauge to a 70° angle. Cut a 10¾-inch-long piece from each end of the strip *(right)*. The piece between the cuts will be the drop-leaf support; the two end pieces will be glued back onto the side rail *(step 2)*. Make the other support the same way.

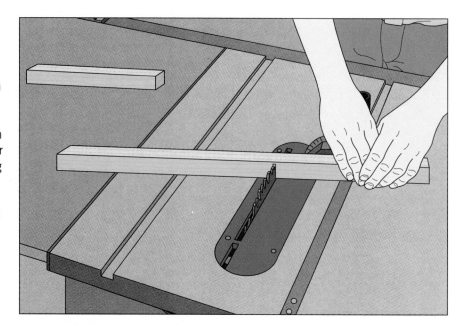

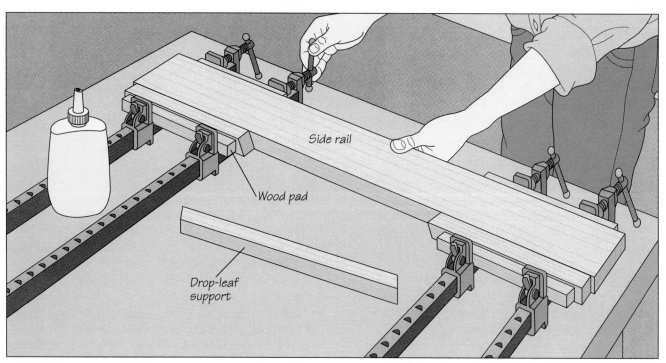

Side rail

Wood pad

Drop-leaf support

2 Reassembling the side rails

Lay four bar clamps on a work surface and set one of the side rails on top. Spread glue on the contacting edges of the outside strips you cut in step 1 and the rails, and press the strips in place. The rail should extend beyond the end of the strips by about ⅛ inch—the width of the saw cuts made in step 1. (The rails will be trimmed later.) Protecting the stock with wood pads, tighten the clamps until a thin glue bead squeezes out of the joints *(above)*. Immediately position the drop-leaf support between the strips to ensure that it butts against the strips; slide the strips along the rail, if necessary. Repeat with the other side rail, then trim the ends of both rails flush.

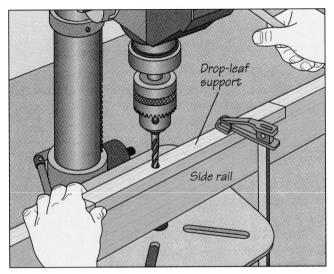

3 Preparing the side rails for the drop-leaf supports
Mark the dowel holes on the top edges of the drop-leaf supports, locating them about 4 inches to one side of the middle. Offsetting the dowels in this way will allow the longer end of the supports to rotate under the leaves. Install a ⅜-inch bit in your drill press and adjust the drilling depth to the dowel length—about 2 inches. Then position the support on its side rail, clamp the assembly to the machine table with the marked point under the bit and, steadying the rail on edge with one hand, drill the hole *(above)*. Repeat for the other side rail.

4 Installing the supports on the rails
Dab some glue into the holes in the rails and tap a dowel into each hole. Once the adhesive has cured, slip the drop-leaf supports onto the dowels *(above)*. Use a chisel to trim the dowels flush with the tops of the supports, if necessary.

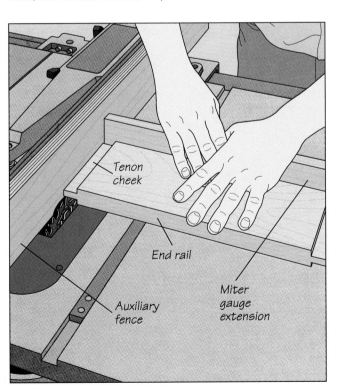

5 Sawing the tenons on the rails
Install a dado head slightly wider than the length of the tenons —¾ inch—on your table saw. (The tenon should be ⅛ inch shorter than the depth of the mortise you chopped in the leg on page 69.) Screw a board as an extension to your miter gauge, then attach an auxiliary fence and raise the dado head to notch it. To cut the tenon cheeks, butt one of the rails against the fence and the miter gauge and feed it face down. Turn the rail over and repeat the cut on the other side, test-fitting the tenon in the leg mortise and raising the blades until the fit is snug. (A loose tenon is difficult to correct, so err or the side of tightness when first adjusting the height of the blades.) Next, cut tenon cheeks at the other end *(left)* and repeat for each rail. Then line up the leg with the rail and mark the final width of the tenon, using the mortise as a guide. Flip the rail on edge and adjust the saw blade to the proper height to trim the width of the tenon. Again, test-fit until the tenon fits snugly in the mortise and the tops of the rail and leg are flush. Now prepare the drawer rail and the kicker the same way. Before assembling the legs and rails, remember to prepare the rails for the wood buttons *(page 93)* that will hold the top in place.

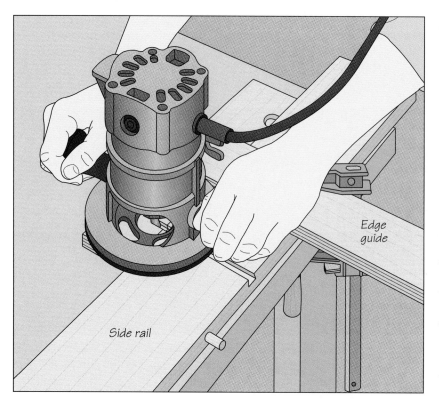

Side rail

Edge guide

6 Preparing the side rails for the cross rail
Joined to the side rails with sliding dovetails, the cross rail adds strength to the table structure and also anchors the corner strips that hold the drawer supports. With the ends of the side rails aligned, mark a cutting line across the middle of the inside faces of both rails. Cut the dovetail sockets with a router in two steps. Start by installing a ¼-inch straight bit in the tool and setting the cutting depth to reach your final depth—½ inch—in two or more passes. Set one of the side rails inside-face up on a work surface, align the bit with your cutting line, and clamp a T square jig—an edge guide with a fence fixed to it at 90°—against the router's base plate so the jig fence butts against the edge of the rail. Rout the slot, then increase the cutting depth and make another pass. Switch to a ½-inch dovetail bit, set the depth at ½ inch, and make a last cut *(left)*. Repeat on the other side rail, making sure to press the router base plate against the edge guide for each pass.

ASSEMBLING THE LEGS AND RAILS

1 Gluing the legs to the drawer rail, kicker, and end rail
Sand the inside faces of the legs and rails, then spread glue on the contacting surfaces between the kicker, drawer rail and one pair of legs. Fit the joints together and secure them with two bar clamps, aligning the bars with the rail and kicker. Using wood pads to protect the stock and distribute the clamping pressure, tighten the clamps gradually until a little adhesive squeezes out of the joints *(right)*. Repeat the procedure to assemble the remaining two legs and the end rail.

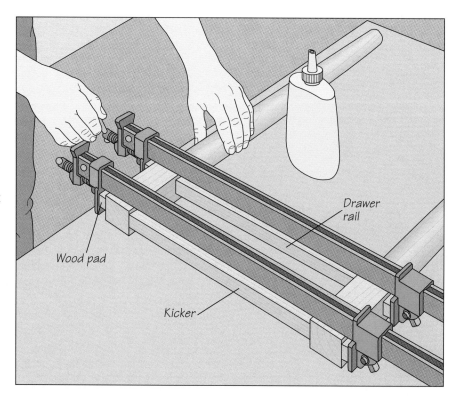

Wood pad

Kicker

Drawer rail

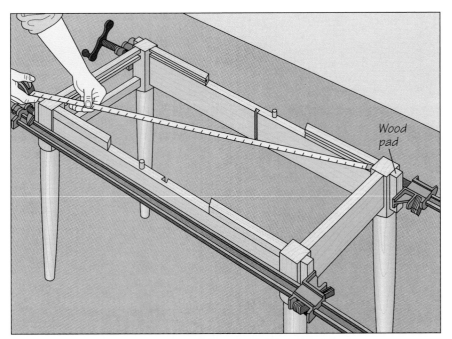

2 Gluing the side rails to the legs

Once the glue has cured, remove the clamps and apply adhesive to the leg mortises and side rail tenons. Fit the joints together and install two bar clamps to secure the assembly, aligning the bars with the side rails. Use wood pads as long as the tenon width to distribute clamping pressure. As soon as you have tightened both clamps, use a tape measure to check the assembly for square *(left)*, measuring the distance between opposite corners; the two measurements should be equal. If not, install another bar clamp across the longer of the two diagonals, setting the clamp jaws on those already in place. Tighten the clamp a little at a time, measuring as you go until the two diagonals are equal.

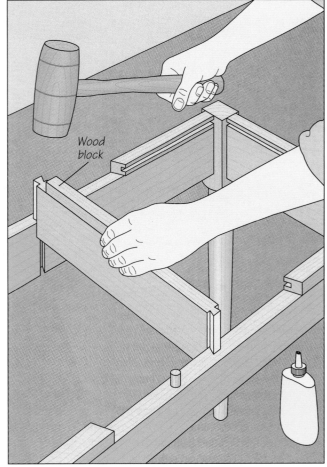

3 Making and installing the cross rail

With the same dovetail bit in your router used to cut the sockets in the side rails *(page 72)*, mount the tool in a table. Set the cutting depth to make the dovetails slightly shorter than the depth of the sockets. Position the fence so that one-half of the cutter projects beyond its face. Feed the cross rail on end across the table, pressing it against the fence. Turn the rail around to complete the dovetail *(above)* and repeat the cuts at the other end of the rail. Test-fit the joints and adjust the fence and make additional cuts, if necessary. Once the fit is snug, spread glue on the dovetails and in the sockets and slide the rail into place, tapping it with a mallet; use a wood block to protect the stock *(right)*. The edges of the cross rail should lie flush with those of the side rails.

MAKING AND INSTALLING THE DRAWER

1 Preparing the drawer for the bottom
Cut the front, back, and sides of the drawer to fit into the opening in the table. The back is narrower than the other pieces to allow the bottom to slide into place after the drawer is glued up. Cut the through dovetails joining the pieces *(page 130)*, then cut the grooves for the bottom panel in the front and side pieces on your table saw. Position the fence so the groove will pass through the middle of the bottom-most tails on the drawer sides and set the blade height to one-half the stock thickness. Use a push stick to feed the pieces face down across the saw table, while pressing the stock against the fence. Repeat on the remaining pieces, then move the fence away from the blade by the thickness of the kerf and repeat on all three boards *(right)*. Test-fit your bottom panel—typically ¼-inch plywood—in the grooves and widen them, if necessary.

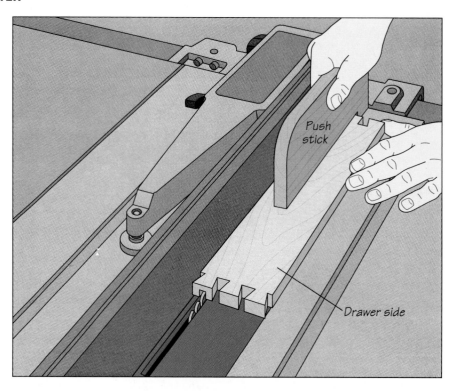

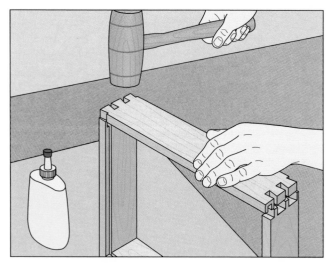

2 Assembling the drawer
Spread glue on the contacting surfaces of the pins and tails, then tap the four boards together using a wooden mallet *(above)*. Clamp the drawer, positioning the clamps to push the tails into the pins. Check the drawer for square *(page 73)*. Once the adhesive has cured, remove the clamps and slide the bottom panel into place. Then drive a few finishing nails through the panel and into the bottom edge of the drawer back to fix it in position.

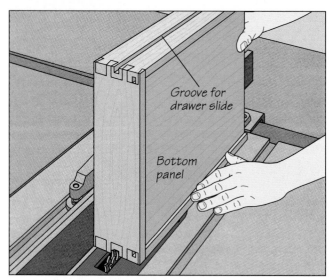

3 Preparing the drawer for the slides
Install a dado head on your table saw and adjust its width to accommodate the drawer slides you will use—typically ⅝ inch thick. Set the cutting height at ⅜ inch and position the rip fence to cut the groove in the middle of the drawer sides. Feed the drawer side-down, holding the edges flush against the fence. Turn the drawer over to cut the groove in the other side *(above)*.

4 Installing the corner strips and drawer slides

Hold the drawer in position in the table and mark the position of the grooves in its sides on the legs and rails. Cut a corner strip for each corner of the drawer *(page 104)*, making the dadoes as wide as the grooves. Screw two corner strips flush against the side rail and leg at the drawer front and use clamps to hold the two remaining strips flush against the side rail and cross rail at the drawer back; the dadoes in all four strips should line up with the groove marks. Cut two drawer slides to span the gap between the dadoes along the side rails, less $\frac{1}{16}$ inch for clearance. Notch the front end to fit around the legs, then slip the slides into the dadoes *(right)*.

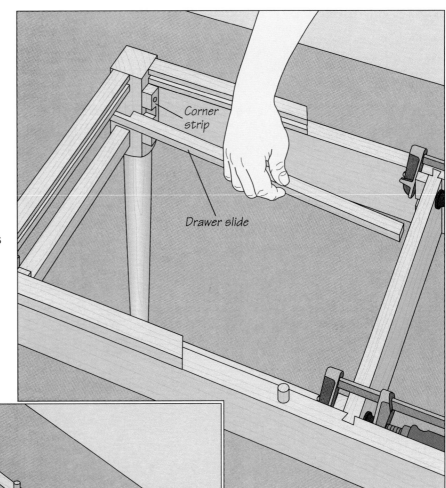

Corner strip

Drawer slide

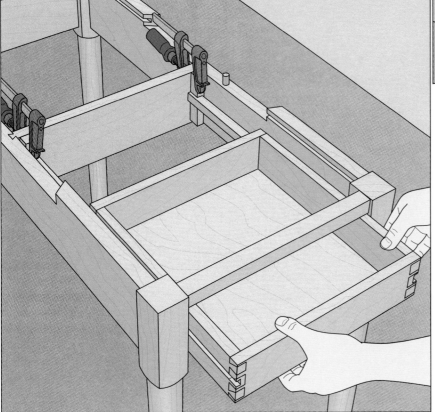

5 Installing the drawer

Slide the drawer into position *(left)*. It should move smoothly and sit centered and level in its opening. If not, loosen the clamps holding the back-end corner strips and adjust the height of the strips, as necessary. When the fit is fine, screw the back end strips to the cross rail.

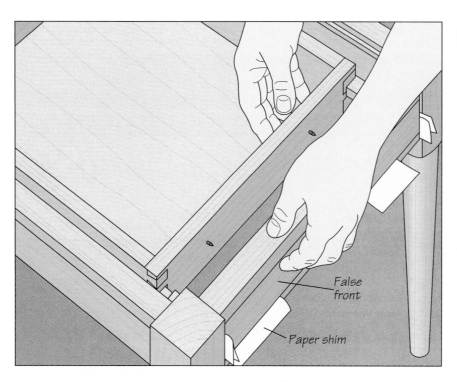

False front

Paper shim

6 Attaching the false front
Set the drawer face-up on a work surface and drive two brads into the front, leaving the heads protruding. Then snip off the heads with pliers. Install the drawer in the table, cut the false front to size and place it between the drawer rail and kicker, using slips of paper as shims to hold it precisely centered and level. Steadying the false front with one hand, slide the drawer toward the board *(left)* and firmly press the brads against it; the pointed ends of the nails will punch impressions in the wood, allowing you to reposition the false front at glue up. Spread adhesive on the back of the false front and clamp it to the drawer with the two brads resting in their impressions.

ATTACHING THE TOP

1 Shaping the top and leaves
The leaves are fastened to the tabletop with rule joints, in which the top's rounded-over edge mates with a cove cut along the edge of the leaf *(inset)*. Start by rounding over the edges of the top, using a piloted round-over bit in a router. To shape the leaves, install a piloted cove bit whose diameter and profile match the round-over bit, then mount the router in a table. (The two bits are often sold as a set.) To support the leaves during the cut, clamp a featherboard to the fence above the cutter. Align the fence with the bit's pilot bearing so the cutting width will equal one-half the cutter diameter. Set the depth of cut to reach the final depth in several passes. Feed one leaf into the bit, bracing its edge against the fence *(right)*. After each pass, test-fit the pieces; continue cutting until the top and leaf mesh with a slight gap between the two. Repeat the process on the other leaf.

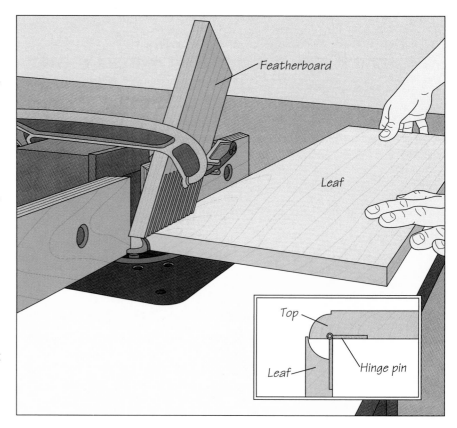

Featherboard

Leaf

Top

Leaf

Hinge pin

2 Attaching the leaves to the top

Join the leaves to the top by installing rule-joint hinges on the underside of the pieces. Set the top and leaves face down on a work surface, then mark lines along the edges of the top in line with the start of each round-over cut, known as the fillet. Install three hinges for each leaf: one in the middle of the joint and one 5 inches from each end. With a paper shim inserted between the leaf and top, position a hinge leaf against the top and the other against the leaf at each hinge location so the pin is aligned with the fillet line, then outline the hinge. Chisel out the mortises, using a wider-blade tool to cut the mortises for the hinge leaves *(page 113)* and a narrower chisel to cut the slots for the pins *(right)*. Screw the hinges in place.

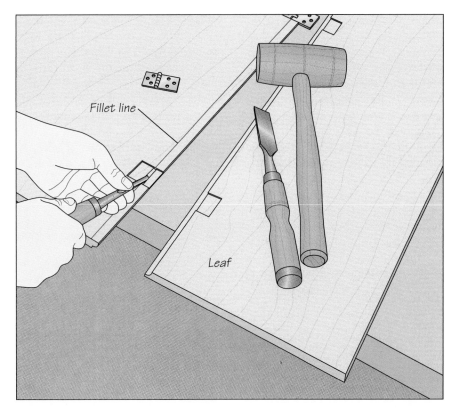

Fillet line

Leaf

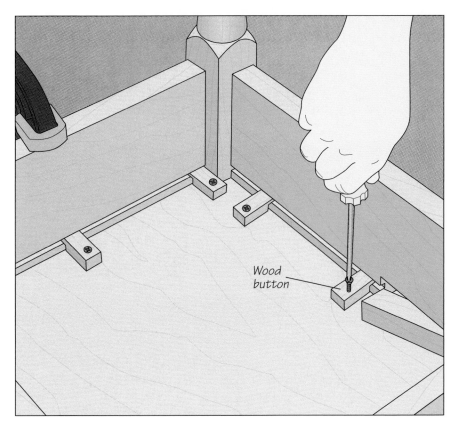

Wood button

3 Attaching the top to the table rails

The top is fastened to the rails with wood buttons; screwed to the top, the buttons feature lips that fit into grooves cut into the rails, providing a secure connection while allowing for wood movement. Make sure the drop-leaf supports are in place on the side rails, then place the top face down on a work surface and clamp the leg-and-rail assembly in position on top. Make a button for every 6 inches of rail length *(page 101)*. Spacing them about 6 inches apart and leaving a ⅛-inch gap between the bottom of the grooves and the lipped ends of the buttons, screw the buttons in place *(left)*.

CANDLE STAND

In an era before electricity, the Shakers depended on candles to see them though the hours of darkness. These diligent workers could not allow late sunrises or early dusks to interfere with their labor. Candle stands were light, stable, and easy to transport. Although candle stands were not a Shaker invention, the furniture makers in their communities elevated this commonplace item to its most refined expression.

The elegance of the candle stand's tripod design sacrifices some strength. Because of the angle at which they splay out, the legs are subjected to a great deal of racking stress which pulls them away from the column. The Shakers compensated for this weakness in several ways. The most important was attaching the legs to the column with sliding dovetails—very strong and durable joints. Some Shaker candle stands have survived 150 years and are as sturdy as the day they were made. To give the legs added strength, a metal plate, known as a "spider," is nailed to the base of the column and legs. The design of the legs also fortifies the stand. They are $^3/_8$ inch thicker at the top, which makes the dovetails that much stronger. Also, the Shakers cut the legs so the grain runs along their length, helping them resist stress.

Despite the simple appearance of the candle stand shown above, the table relies on precise joinery. Positioned exactly 120° apart, the three legs are attached to the column with sliding dovetails, cut with angled shoulders to sit snugly against the column.

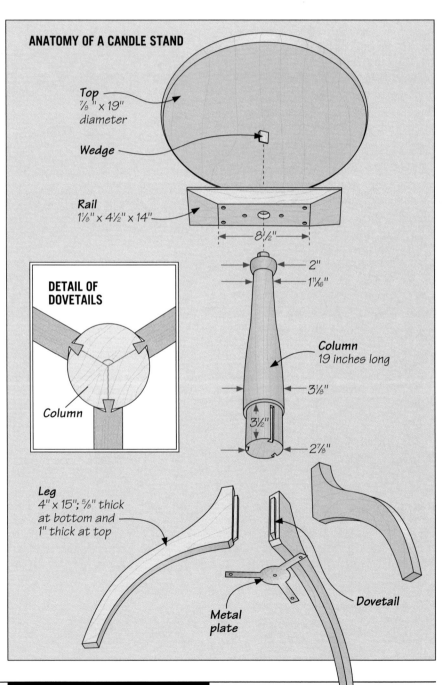

ANATOMY OF A CANDLE STAND

Top
$^7/_8$" × 19" diameter

Wedge

Rail
$1^1/_8$" × $4^1/_2$" × 14"

8½"

2"

$1^{11}/_{16}$"

DETAIL OF DOVETAILS

Column

Column
19 inches long

3⅛"

3½"

2⅞"

Leg
4" × 15"; ⅝" thick at bottom and 1" thick at top

Metal plate

Dovetail

CIRCLE-CUTTING JIG

To cut the circular top of a candle stand on your band saw, use the shop-built circle-cutting jig shown at right. Refer to the illustration for suggested dimensions.

Rout a ⅜-inch-deep dovetail channel in the middle of the jig base, then use a table saw to rip a thin board with a bevel along both edges to produce a bar that slides smoothly in the channel. (Set the saw blade angle by measuring the angle of the channel edges.) Cut out the notch on the band saw, then screw the support arms to the underside of the jig base, spacing them to hug the sides of the band saw table when the jig is in position. Drill two holes through the bottom of the dovetail channel in the jig base, 1 inch and 3 inches from the unnotched end; also bore two holes through the bar as shown.

To prepare the workpiece, mark the circumference and center of the circle on its underside. Then use the band saw to cut off the four corners of the panel to keep it from hitting

the clamps that secure the jig. Next, make a release cut from the edge of the panel to the marked circumference, then veer off to the edge. Screw the pivot bar to the center of the workpiece through one of the bar's holes, leaving the screw loose enough to pivot the panel.

Turn the workpiece over and mark the point where the blade contacted the circumference during the release cut. Clamp the jig base to

the band saw table, making sure the support arms are butted against the table's edges. Slide the pivot bar into the channel in the base and pivot the panel until the marked contact point touches the blade. Screw through one of the holes in the jig base to lock the pivot bar in place *(below, left)*. Turn on the saw and pivot the workpiece into the blade in a clockwise direction *(below, right)*, feeding the piece until the cut is completed.

Jig base
¾" x 20" x 24"

Notch
¾" x 7"

Screw holes

Dovetail channel
⅜" x ¾" x 24"

Support arm
1" x 3" x 8"

Sliding pivot bar
¾" x 24"

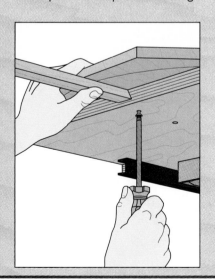

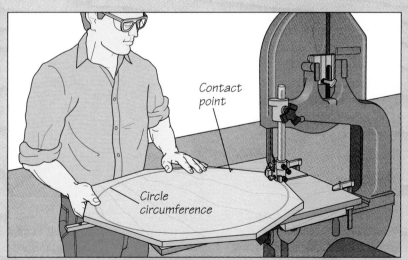

Contact point

Circle circumference

PREPARING THE TOP AND RAIL

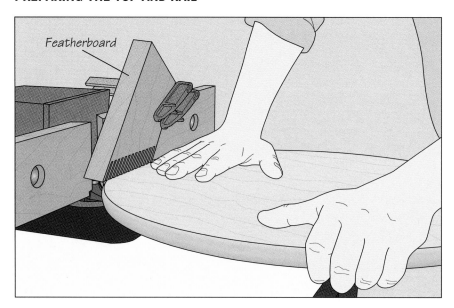

Featherboard

1 Preparing the top
Once the top of the candle stand has been cut *(page 79)*, shape its circumference on a router table in two steps. Start by installing a piloted ½-inch radius bit in a router and mounting the tool in a table. Align the fence with the bit's pilot bearing and clamp a featherboard to the fence to support the top during the cut. Holding the top face-up and flat on the table, press the edge against the fence and rotate the stock into the bit *(left)*. Continue pivoting the top until the entire circumference is shaped, then switch to a piloted ¼-inch radius bit, turn the workpiece over, and repeat to shape its top side.

2 Making the rail
Referring to the anatomy illustration on page 78, cut the rail that will connect the column to the tabletop, then bore a mortise in the center of the rail to accept the tenon you will turn at the top of the column; a 1-inch-diameter hole is typical. Bevel the ends and edges of the rail on your table saw. Attach an auxiliary fence and position the fence to the left of the blade for a ¼-inch cutting width. Raise the blade to its maximum setting, adjust the angle to about 75°, and clamp a guide block to the rail to ride along the top of the fence. Mark a line across the face of the rail slightly above the height of the blade as a reminder to keep your hands well above the blade. Feed the rail into the blade on end, keeping it flush against the fence and pushing it forward with the guide block. Repeat the cut at the other end of the rail *(right)*. Then bevel the long edges by adjusting the blade angle to 45°. Sand the rail smooth.

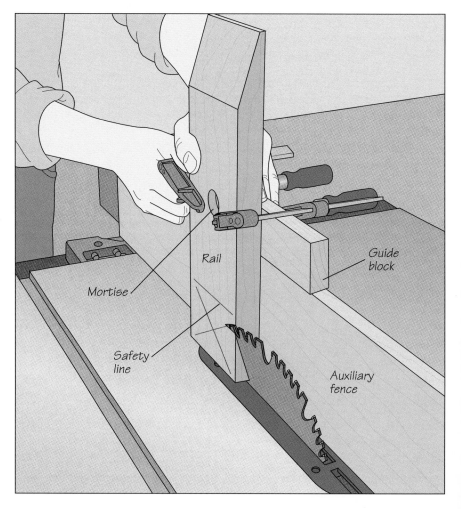

Rail

Guide block

Mortise

Safety line

Auxiliary fence

MAKING THE COLUMN

1 Turning the column

Mount a 3½-inch-square blank on your lathe and turn it with a roughing gouge followed by a spindle gouge, leaving a lip and enough stock near the bottom for the leg sockets. To help you produce the proper shape, refer to the anatomy illustration *(page 78)* and fashion yourself a template, as you would to turn a drop-leaf table leg *(page 69)*. Use a parting tool to turn the rail tenon at the top of the column, periodically checking its diameter with outside calipers *(right)*. Smooth the column with progressively finer grits of sandpaper.

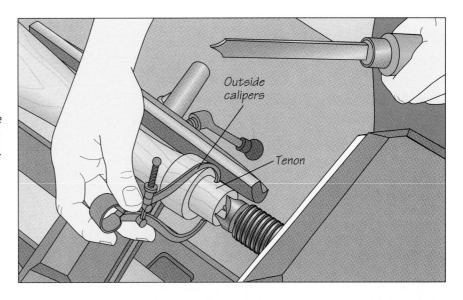

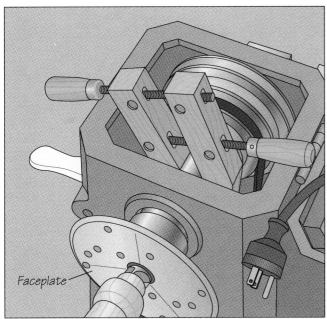

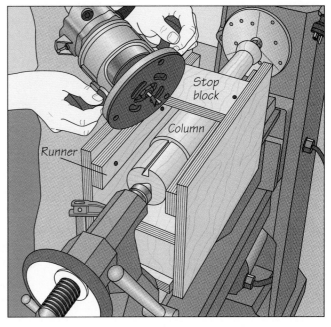

2 Routing the dovetail sockets

Unplug the lathe and cut the sockets, using a router and a shop-made jig consisting of a ¾-inch plywood box clamped to the lathe bed. Make the inside width of the box as wide as the router base plate, attaching the runners so the router bit will cut the sockets with its base plate sitting on them. Next, mark the three socket locations on the column, spacing them 120° apart. Also mark the top ends of the sockets, 3⁷⁄₁₆ inches from the bottom of the column. Transfer the socket marks to the lathe faceplate, then rotate the column by hand until one of the marks on the faceplate is vertical and immobilize the drive shaft with a handscrew *(above, left)*. Cut each socket in two steps, starting with a ¼-inch straight bit. Adjust the cutting depth to about ½ inch and, aligning the bit with the socket end mark, butt a stop block against the router base plate. Screw the block to the jig. Holding the router in both hands, feed the bit into the column at the bottom and guide the tool along the runners until the base plate contacts the stop block. Repeat with a ¼-inch dovetail bit *(above, right)*. To cut the two remaining sockets, rotate the column until the socket mark for each cut is vertical.

MAKING THE LEGS

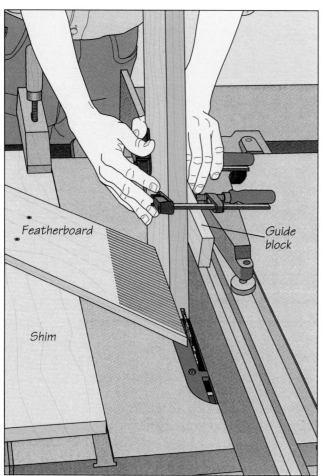

Featherboard

Guide block

Shim

1 Cutting the dovetail cheeks
Referring to the illustration below, fashion a template for the legs. The grain should follow the slope of the leg, the top and bottom ends must be perpendicular, and the spread of the legs must be less than the diameter of the top. Once the template is complete, saw along the top end of the leg on the band saw. Next, cut the dovetails in the legs in two steps, cutting the cheeks on your table saw and the shoulders by hand. Adjust the table saw's blade angle to match that of the sockets you cut in the column and set the cutting height to slightly less than the depth of the sockets. Outline the dovetails on the edge of one leg blank and, holding the blank on end on the saw table, align a cutting mark with the blade. Butt the rip fence against the stock and lock it in place. Clamp a shimmed featherboard to the table and a guide block to the blank. Make a pass to cut one cheek *(left)*, then rotate the blank and feed the opposite face along the fence to saw the other. Check the resulting dovetail against a socket in the column. If necessary, adjust the cutting width or blade angle or height and make another set of passes. Repeat for the remaining dovetails.

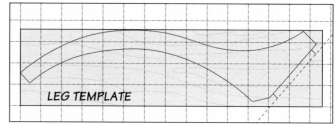

LEG TEMPLATE

2 Cutting the angled shoulders
The shoulders of the leg dovetails must be cut at an angle so they lie snugly against the column (see the illustration on page 78). Once the dovetail cheeks are all cut, clamp a blank to a work surface with the cheeks extending off the table. Then use a backsaw to cut the shoulders at a slightly sharper angle than the curvature of the column *(right)*. Test-fit the dovetail in its socket and trim the socket, if necessary, until you get a suitable fit. Repeat for the remaining dovetails.

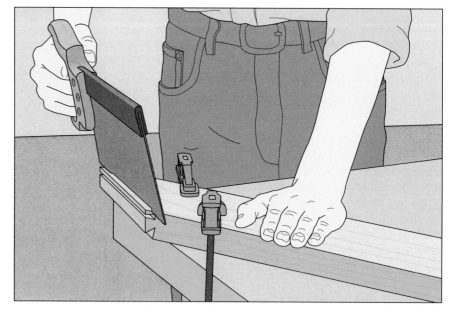

3 Shaping the legs

Cut out the legs of the candle stand on your band saw, then smooth their surfaces using a sanding block or a spindle sander *(right)*.

4 Trimming the dovetails

Trim off the top ¾ inch of each dovetail on the legs. This will hide the tops of the dovetails from view when they are pushed all the way into their sockets. Clamp the leg upright in your bench vise and mark a line on the dovetail ¾ inch from the top end. Then hold a ¼-inch chisel vertically to score the dovetail on your marked line, cutting to the shoulder. Next, holding the chisel bevel up and parallel to the dovetail shoulders, push the blade along the surface to pare away the wood in thin shavings *(left)*. Periodically test-fit the leg against the column until the shoulders rest flush against the surface.

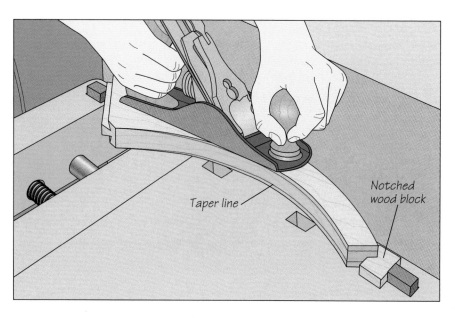

5 Tapering the legs
To give the legs an elegant appearance without sacrificing strength, taper them with a bench plane from a thickness of 1 inch at the top to ⅝ inch at the bottom. Mark taper lines along the inside edges of each leg as a planing guide. Then secure the leg face up on your bench, using a notched wood block to fix the bottom end in place. To avoid damaging your plane blade, make sure the bench dogs and the wood block are below the level of the top taper line. Starting near the top of the leg, feed the plane along the surface, increasing the downward pressure as you approach the bottom *(left)*. Continue until you cut to the taper line, then turn the leg over on the bench and repeat the process.

ASSEMBLING THE TABLE

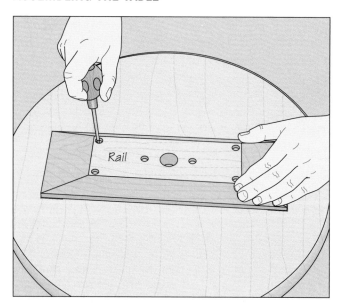

1 Attaching the rail to the column
Start by drilling six countersunk screw holes through the rail; it will be less cumbersome to prepare the rail for the top before joining the rail and column. Locate one hole in each corner of the flat face of the rail's underside and one on each side of the mortise. Then set the top face down on a work surface and center the rail on top, making sure the grain of the two pieces is perpendicular. Mark the corners of the rail on the top with a pencil and the screw holes with an awl *(above, left)*. To prepare the column for the rail, use a backsaw to slice a kerf for a wedge in the center of the tenon to a depth of about

three-quarters the length of the tenon. Cut the kerf at a right angle to one of the dovetail sockets so the rail will be parallel to one of the legs. Cut the wedge from hardwood about 1 inch long and ⅛ inch thick at the base, tapering it to a point. To fasten the rail to the column, spread glue on their contacting surfaces and fit the pieces together with the kerf in the column tenon perpendicular to the grain of the rail. Then, holding the column upright on a work surface, apply glue in the kerf and on the wedge and hammer it in place with a wooden mallet *(above, right)*. Trim the wedge flush with the end of the tenon.

2 Fastening the legs to the column

Spread glue evenly on the dovetails and in the sockets. Then, setting the rail flat on a work surface, slide the legs into place and tap them into final position with a wooden mallet *(right)*. To strengthen the assembly, add a three-armed spider cut from sheet metal *(page 78)*.

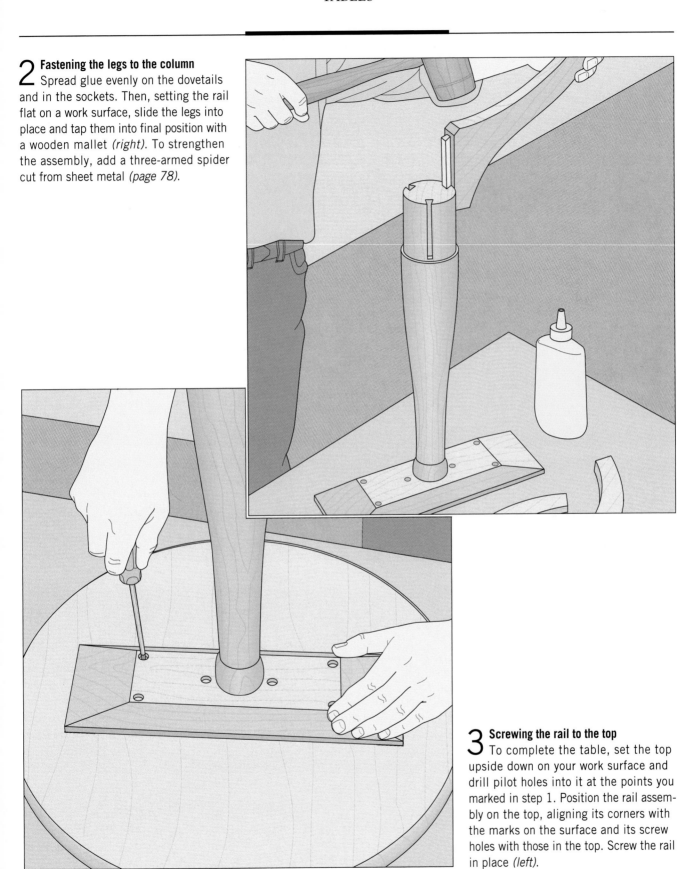

3 Screwing the rail to the top

To complete the table, set the top upside down on your work surface and drill pilot holes into it at the points you marked in step 1. Position the rail assembly on the top, aligning its corners with the marks on the surface and its screw holes with those in the top. Screw the rail in place *(left)*.

PIE SAFE

A nail set and hammer punch a hole through a tin panel for a pie safe. To ensure that all the panels will be identical, each blank is placed on a backup panel and a paper template with the desired pattern is taped in place on top.

Pie safes were once common in American kitchens. The one shown at left reflects the Shaker devotion to utility. The cabinets were essentially large bread boxes, designed to store baked goods made and consumed by Shaker families. That the cabinets are elegant and attractive is, in a sense, coincidental, for it is a reflection of the Shakers' spare and utilitarian ethic rather than an expression of esthetics.

All property and goods in Shaker communities were owned collectively, to be used as needed. Since belongings were not considered private, latches and locks on the doors of a pie safe would have been superfluous. Doors sported simple wooden knobs and mating rabbets cut along the inside faces of their stiles so they would close flush and tightly together. The most clever feature of the safe lies in the design of the tin door panels. The cabinets had to keep rodents and insects from getting inside while allowing enough air to circulate to prevent the food from becoming stale. With the use of tin door panels, Shaker furniture makers solved both problems at once. The small holes in the panels permitted the passage of air. And, by punching the holes from the inside out, they created sharp edges on the outside that discouraged the intrusion of vermin. For maximum ventilation, Shaker pie safes traditionally featured tin panels on the sides as well as in the doors.

One of the charming elements of these pieces is the hole pattern. The designs were sometimes abstract and sometimes pineapple-shaped or floral, as in the example shown on page 86. But again, these details were not primarily intended to be ornamental or flamboyant. The panels had to be perforated, so the Shakers chose to punch the holes symmetrically to avoid an unnecessarily ornate or otherwise distracting appearance.

Pie safes were traditionally made from cherry, although communities where hardwoods were scarce frequently resorted to pine. This chapter provides detailed step-by-step instructions for building a Shaker-inspired safe, beginning with cutting the rails, stiles and panels for the cabinet *(page 90)* and continuing through gluing up the case *(page 97)*, making and installing the shelves *(page 104)*, and assembling the doors *(page 106)*. Although rooted in the Shaker tradition, a pie safe like this one would be a perfect addition to any modern, country-style kitchen.

With its sturdy frame-and-panel construction, adjustable shelving, and perforated tin door panels, the pie safe shown at left is ideal for storing baked goods. In a modern incarnation, the safe could be used as an entertainment center, with plenty of space for audio or video equipment.

ANATOMY OF A PIE SAFE

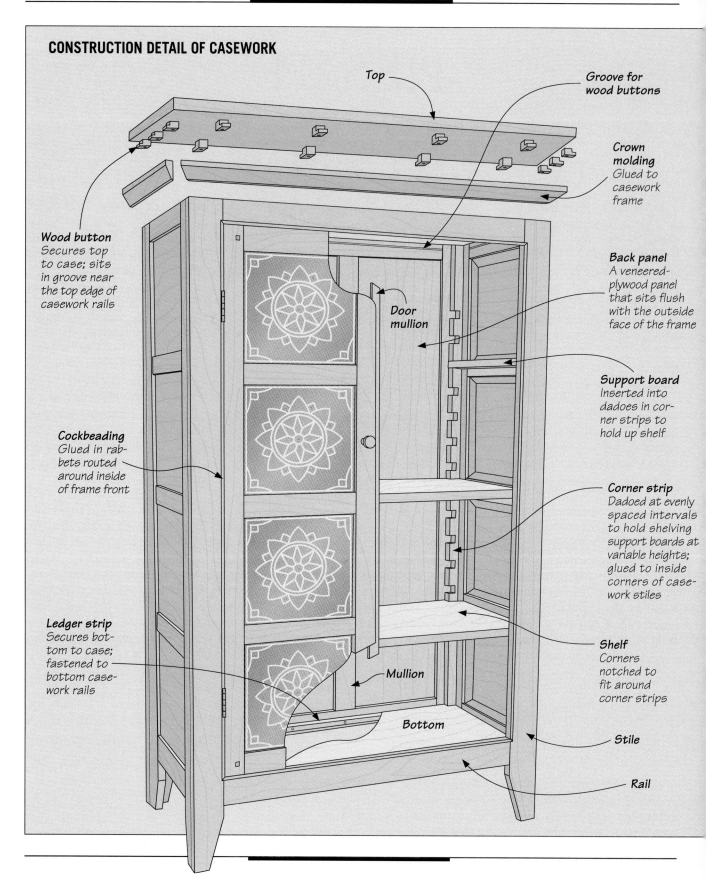

CONSTRUCTION DETAIL OF CASEWORK

Top

Groove for wood buttons

Crown molding
Glued to casework frame

Wood button
Secures top to case; sits in groove near the top edge of casework rails

Back panel
A veneered-plywood panel that sits flush with the outside face of the frame

Door mullion

Cockbeading
Glued in rabbets routed around inside of frame front

Support board
Inserted into dadoes in corner strips to hold up shelf

Corner strip
Dadoed at evenly spaced intervals to hold shelving support boards at variable heights; glued to inside corners of casework stiles

Ledger strip
Secures bottom to case; fastened to bottom casework rails

Mullion

Shelf
Corners notched to fit around corner strips

Bottom

Stile

Rail

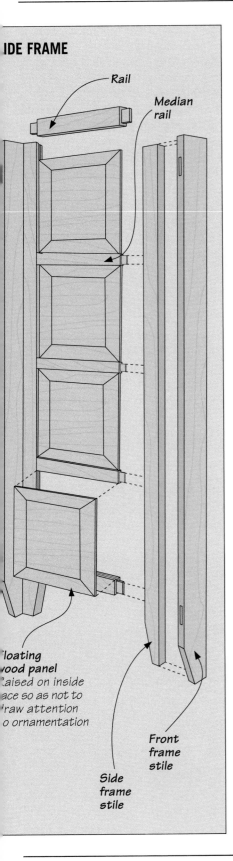

IDE FRAME

Rail

Median rail

Floating wood panel
Raised on inside ace so as not to raw attention o ornamentation

Front frame stile

Side frame stile

The pie safe featured in this chapter comprises four frames joined at the corners. Each frame is made with rails and stiles connected with mortise-and-tenons. The side frames are grooved to house floating wood panels. The back frame is divided in half by a mullion and is rabbeted around the inside edges to accommodate fixed back panels. The front frame is made the same way as the sides, with two hinges holding each door to its stiles. To assemble the safe, the side frames are built first and then glued together with the front and back rails.

The top and bottom are solid panels of edge-glued boards. The top is held in place by wood buttons and the bottom is fastened to ledger strips. The solid-wood shelves sit on support boards that are held by corner strips. The inside edges of the front frame are rabbeted to accommodate cockbeading.

CUTTING LIST

PIECE		QTY	L	W	TH
Frame stiles	(sides)	4	60"	2⅜"	¾"
	(front and back)	4	60"	3"	¾"
Frame rails*	(front and back)	4	31½"	2⅝"	¾"
	(side, top, and bottom)	4	14½"	2⅝"	¾"
	(side, median)	6	14½"	1¾"	¾"
Mullion*		1	50"	2⁵⁄₁₆"	¾"
Wood panels		8	13½"	12¼"	½"
Top		1	40"	20"	¾"
Bottom		1	34"	16¼"	¾"
Door stiles		4	48½"	2"	⅞"
Door rails*	(top and bottom)	4	15"	2"	⅞"
	(median)	6	12"	1⅝"	⅞"
Crown molding		1	75⅞"	1⅛"	⅞"
Corner strips		2	54¼"	1¾"	1"
Shelves		2	33¾"	16⅛"	⅞"
Back panels		2	49⅜"	14⁵⁄₁₆"	¼"
Shelf support boards		4	16½"	¾"	¾"
Cockbeading		1	161"	½"	¼"

*Note: Measurements include tenon lengths.

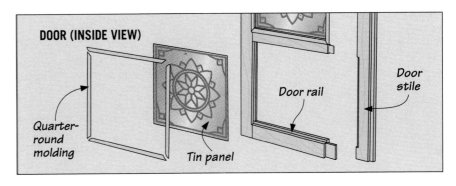

DOOR (INSIDE VIEW)

Quarter-round molding

Tin panel

Door rail

Door stile

MAKING THE CASEWORK FRAMES

The first step in building a pie safe is to cut and prepare the frame stiles, as shown below, and join them in pairs to form the corners of the cabinet. All of the mortises are cut in the stiles, then the tenons are cut at the ends of the rails. As shown on page 92, the best method for cutting the blind tenons is by hand—with a backsaw and a miter box. Next, the frames are dry-assembled and grooves are routed along their inside edges for the floating wood panels (*page 93*). Finally, the top rails are grooved on the table saw to accommodate the wood buttons that will secure the top.

A hollow chisel mortiser drills a mortise in a pie safe frame stile. The mortise will accommodate a rail tenon. Although the Shakers would have painstakingly chiseled out their mortises by hand, as shown on page 91, using a power tool is quick and accurate.

PREPARING THE STILES

1 Tapering the stiles
Referring to the cutting list on page 89, cut the frame stiles to size, then taper their bottom ends. The tapers will give the bottom of the stiles an elegant, leg-like appearance. Clamp one of the stiles face up on a work surface and make one cutting mark on its bottom end 1½ inches from the inside edge and another mark on the edge 5 inches up from the bottom. Join the two marks with a line, then use a rip saw to cut the taper along the line *(right)*. Use the tapered stile as a template to mark cutting lines on the remaining stiles, then taper them the same way. Sand all the cut edges smooth.

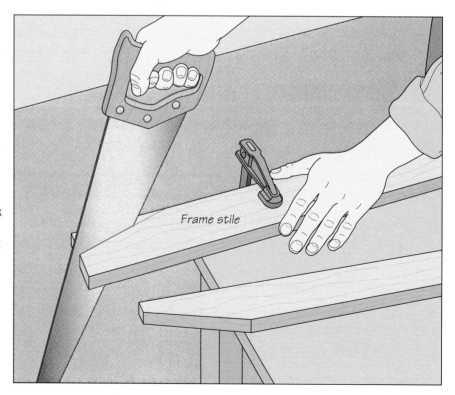

Frame stile

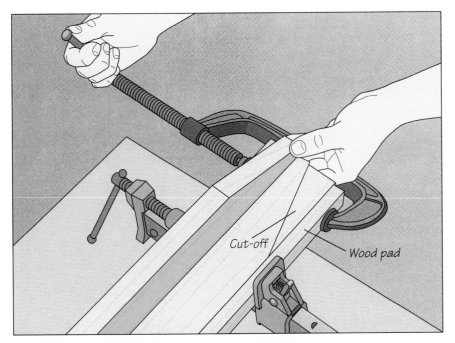

2 Gluing up the stiles

Glue the stiles together in pairs to form the corner of the pie safe. Remember that the four wider stiles will be used on the front and back of the safe, while the narrower stiles will fit on the sides; this way, the corner joint will only be visible from the sides. Spread some glue on the contacting surfaces of each pair of stiles: the outside edges of the side stiles and the inside faces of the front and back stiles. With the side stile face down on a work surface, secure the joint, spacing the clamps about 12 inches apart; protect the stock and distribute the clamping pressure with wood pads. To secure the joint where the stile has been tapered, use a cut-off from the taper cuts you made in step 1 to square the clamp on the stock *(left)*.

Cut-off

Wood pad

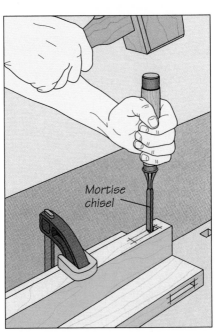

Mortise chisel

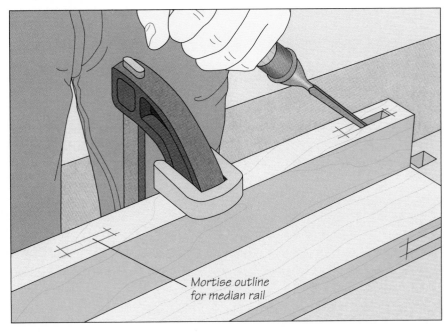

Mortise outline for median rail

3 Cutting the mortises in the stiles

Each stile needs a mortise at the top and bottom to accommodate a rail tenon; you also have to cut three more mortises in each of the side stiles for the median rail tenons. You can use a power tool such as a hollow chisel mortiser *(page 90)* to make the cut, or chisel them out by hand, as shown above. Referring to the anatomy illustration on page 88, outline the mortises on the edges of the stiles, then clamp one of the glued-up stiles to a work surface. Starting at one end of the outline, hold a mortise chisel square to the edge of the stile and strike it with a wooden mallet. Use a chisel the same width as the mortise and be sure the beveled side of the blade is facing the waste. Make another cut ¼ inch from the first *(above, left)*. Continue until you reach the other end of the outline, then lever out the waste to a depth of about ⅞ inch *(above, right)*. Repeat to cut the remaining mortises, then smooth the bottom of the mortises with a lock-mortise chisel.

PREPARING THE RAILS

1 Cutting the tenon cheeks

Outline the tenons at both ends of the rails, marking a shoulder line all around the ends so the length of the tenons will be slightly less than the depth of the mortises you cut in the stiles. Secure one of the rails upright in a vise and cut along the lines on the end of the board with a backsaw until you reach the shoulder line *(right)*. Repeat for the tenon at the other end of the rail and at both ends of the remaining rails.

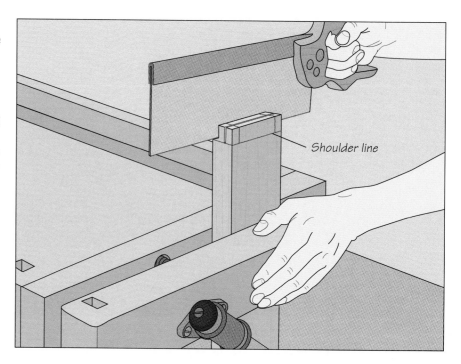

Shoulder line

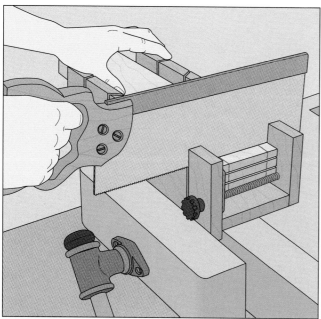

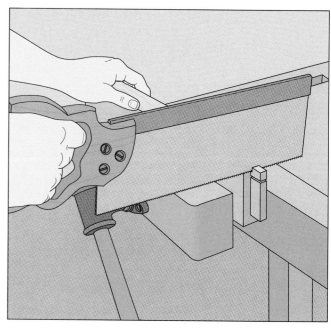

2 Sawing the tenon shoulders

To remove the waste from the tenon cheeks, secure a miter box in the vise, then set the rail on the base of the box, aligning the shoulder line with the 90° slot. Tighten the clamps in the box to hold the rail in position. Slip the backsaw blade into the slot and cut along the shoulder line on the face of the board, stopping when you reach the kerf you cut in step 1 *(above, left)*; turn over the stock and repeat the operation on the other side. To cut away the waste on the edges of the tenon, secure the the rail upright in the vise and saw to the shoulder line on both edges of the rail. Finally, clamp the rail edge up and cut through the shoulder line on both edges of the rail *(above, right)*.

3 Preparing the top rails for wood buttons
Once all the tenons are finished, you will need to cut a groove along the top frame rails of the safe to accommodate the wood buttons that will secure the cabinet top in place. Install a dado head on your table saw, adjust its width to ¼ inch, and set the cutting height at about ⅞ inch. Position the rip fence about ¾ inch from the blades and install two featherboards to support the rails, clamping one to the fence above the dado head and another to the table. Brace the second featherboard with a support board. Feed the rails into the dado head inside-face down and with the top edge pressed against the fence *(right)*. Finish each pass with a push stick.

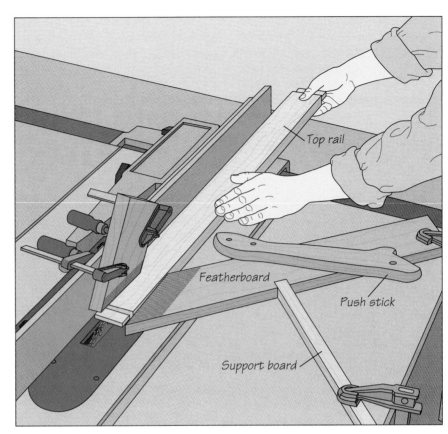

Top rail

Featherboard

Push stick

Support board

PREPARING THE FRAMES FOR FLOATING PANELS

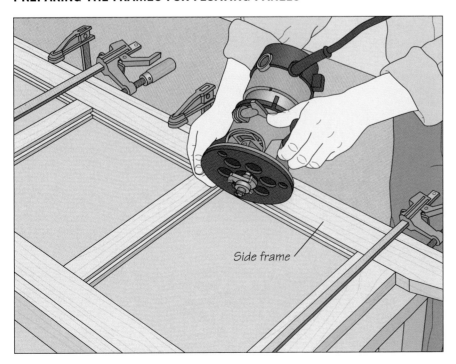

Side frame

Routing the panel grooves
Cut the panel grooves along the inside edges of the side frames with a router and a piloted three-wing slotting cutter. Dry-assemble each side frame and clamp one of them face down on a work surface. Adjust the router's cutting depth to center the groove on the edges of the stock. With a firm grip on the router, turn on the tool and lower the base plate onto the surface. Guide the bit into the stock near one corner of the frame. Once the pilot bearing butts against the edge of the stock, continue the cut in a clockwise direction. Repeat the process for the other panel openings, repositioning the clamps as necessary.

RAISING THE PANELS

Raised panels, with their distinctive beveled edges, evolved as a practical solution to two common problems faced by Shaker cabinetmakers: how to fit thick panels into frames made of thinner stock and how to compensate for wood movement. Beveling the panels allowed them to fit in the grooves in the inside edges of the frames. No adhesive was used, so the panels could swell and shrink with changes in humidity.

Cut the panels ½ inch longer and wider than the openings in the frames. There are several ways of raising panels. Shaker builders likely did the job by hand, using panel-raising planes, as shown in the photo at left. A more common approach, shown below and on the following pages, involves beveling the edges of panels on a router table or table saw.

Most furniture makers other than the Shakers have installed the panels with the raised, central portion facing outward, adding visual interest to their pieces.

Although Shakers in the Western communities, where German influence admitted some decoration, might have done the same, the Shaker creed frowned on extraneous ornamentation. As a result, Shaker pie safes were often built with the flat side of the panels facing out, while the attractive, raised faces are hidden from view on the inside.

A panel-raising plane bevels one end of a wood panel. These hand tools must be used in pairs to raise a panel. Using left- and right-hand models allows the panel to be beveled in the direction of the grain at all times.

RAISING PANELS ON A ROUTER TABLE

Making a raised panel with a router

Install a panel-raising bit in your router and mount the tool in a table. Position the fence in line with the bit's pilot bearing and set the cutting depth at ⅛ inch so that you can reach your final depth in two or more passes. Lower the guard over the bit and turn on the router. To minimize tearout, cut the end grain of the panel first, beveling the top and bottom before the sides. Keep the panel flat on the table inside face down and flush against the fence as you feed it across the bit *(right)*. Repeat the cut at the other end and along both sides. Turn off the router and test-fit one end in a frame groove. If the panel lies less than ¼ inch deep in the groove, increase the cutting depth slightly and make another pass all around. Continue in this fashion until the panel fits properly.

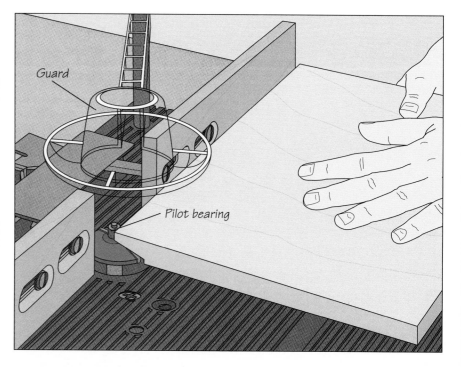

Guard

Pilot bearing

MAKING RAISED PANELS ON A TABLE SAW

1 Beveling the ends

To determine the blade angle for raising the panels, draw a ¼-inch square at the bottom corner of one piece, then mark a line from the inside face of the panel through the inside corner of the square to a point on the bottom edge ⅛ inch from the outside face *(inset)*. Install a 6-inch-wide auxiliary wood fence, hold the panel against the fence and adjust the blade angle until it aligns with the marked line. Next, adjust the blade height until the outside tip of one tooth extends beyond the inside face of the panel, then clamp a guide block to the panel to ride along the top of the fence. Feed the panel into the blade, keeping it flush against the fence while pushing it forward with the guide block *(right)*. Test-fit the cut end in a frame groove. If less than ¼ inch of the panel enters the groove, move the fence a little closer to the blade and make another pass. Repeat the cut at the other end of the panel.

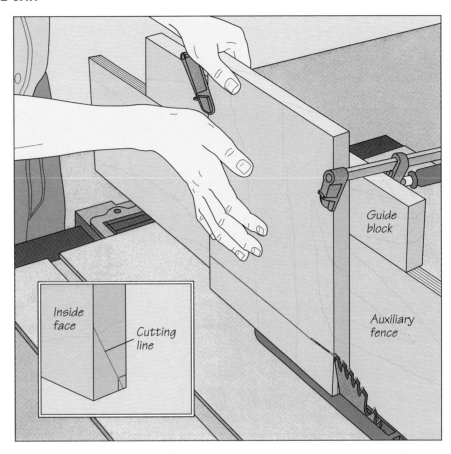

Guide block

Inside face

Cutting line

Auxiliary fence

2 Beveling the sides

Beveling the sides after you have beveled the end grain helps minimize tearout. Set the panel on edge and feed it into the blade, keeping the back flush against the fence. Turn the panel over to cut the remaining edge *(left)*.

BUILD IT YOURSELF

A PANEL-RAISING JIG
FOR THE TABLE SAW

To raise a panel on the table saw with-out adjusting the angle of the blade, use the shop built jig shown at right. Refer to the illustration for suggest-ed dimensions.

Screw the lip along the bottom edge of the angled fence; make sure you position the screws where they will not interfere with the blade. Prop the angled fence against the auxil-iary fence at the same angle as the cutting line marked on a panel *(page 95)*, using a sliding bevel to transfer the angle. Cut triangular supports to fit precisely between the two fences, then fix them in place with screws. Countersink the fasteners so the panel will slide smoothly along the angled fence.

To use the jig, position it on the saw table with the joint between the lip and the angled fence about ⅛ inch from the blade. Butt the table saw's rip fence against the jig's auxil-iary fence and screw the two together. Turn on the saw and crank up the blade slowly to cut a kerf through the lip. Next, seat the panel in the jig and adjust the height of the blade until a single tooth protrudes beyond the front of the panel. Make a test cut in a scrap board the same thickness as the panel and then check its fit in the groove; adjust the position of the fence or blade, if necessary. Then cut the panel, beveling the ends *(right, bottom)* before sawing the sides.

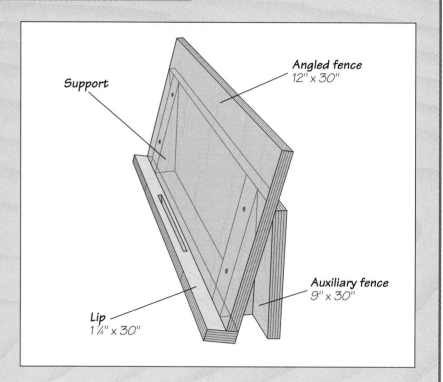

Support

Angled fence
12" x 30"

Auxiliary fence
9" x 30"

Lip
1¼" x 30"

ASSEMBLING THE SAFE

Once all the floating panels are ready, it is time to glue the frames together. Start by fitting the panels into their frames, as shown below, then glue up the rails and stiles, forming the sides of the cabinet *(page 98)*. The next step involves installing the back panel on the frame *(page 99)*.

The pie safe featured in this chapter includes two of the few decorative touches found in Shaker furniture: crown molding and cockbeading around the inside edges of the door openings in the front frame. The molding provides a smooth visual transition from the front and sides to the top of the safe. Although molding might appear to be an extraneous embellishment, the restrained, unadorned design shown is entirely in keeping with the Shaker ideals of simplicity and harmony.

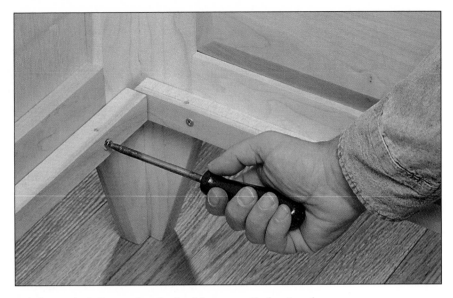

A ledger strip is fastened to the back bottom rail of a pie safe. Once strips have been attached to all four bottom rails, the bottom panel will be screwed to the top edge of the strips.

ASSEMBLING THE SIDE PANELS

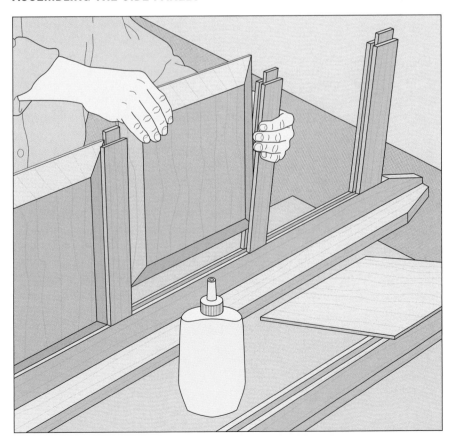

1 Fitting the panels into their frames

Test-assemble the side frames. If a joint is too tight, disassemble the pieces and use a chisel to pare away some wood. Once you are satisfied with the fit, sand any surfaces that will be difficult to reach when the frame has been glued up, and spread adhesive on all the contacting surfaces of the rails and stiles. Do not apply any glue in the panel grooves; the panels must be free to move within the frame. Set one of the stile pairs on a work surface, fit the rail tenons into their mortises, then slip the frames into their grooves *(left)*, tapping them into position with a mallet, if necessary. Fit the opposite stile pair on the rails and clamp the frame *(step 2)*.

2 Clamping the side frames

Set the frame inside-face down on a work surface and secure the mortise-and-tenon joints with bar clamps. Aligning the bars with the rails, tighten the clamps until a glue bead squeezes out of the joints *(right)*. Protect the stiles with wood pads. Use a try square to ensure that the frame remains square as you tighten the clamps. Once the adhesive has cured, remove the clamps and then sand all the wood smooth.

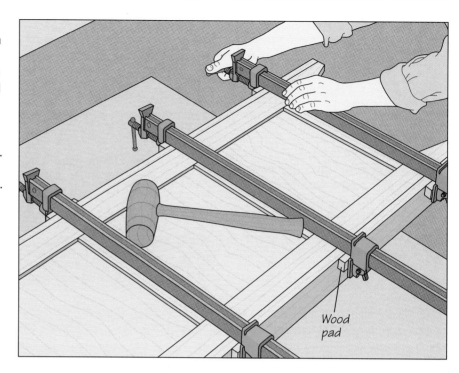

Wood pad

GLUING UP THE SAFE

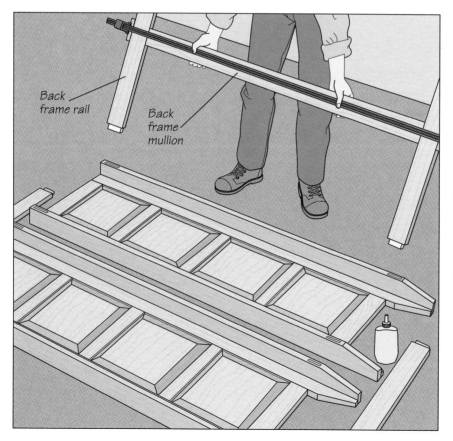

Back frame rail

Back frame mullion

1 Gluing the front and back to the sides

Prepare the rails of the front and back of the pie safe as you would for the sides *(page 92)* and also cut a mullion for the back frame. Cut tenons at the ends of the mullion and rout or chisel out matching mortises on the edges of the back frame rails. Then glue the pieces together, using a long bar clamp to secure the joints. Set the side frames inside-face up on your shop floor and spread some glue on all the contacting surfaces between the side frames and the front and back. Fit the back frame tenons into their mortises in one of the sides *(left)*, then install the front frame the same way. Finally, set the remaining side frame on top.

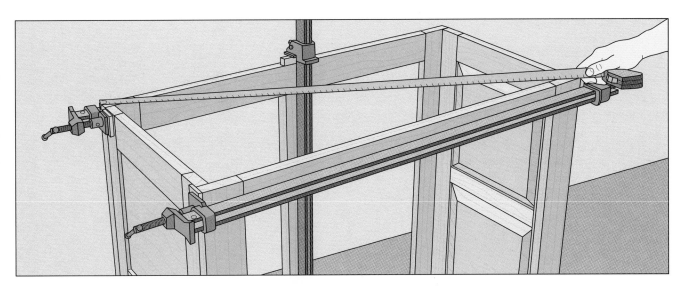

2 Clamping the safe

Carefully set the cabinet upright, working with a helper, if necessary. Use four more bar clamps to secure the sides to the front and back, aligning two clamps with the top rails of the front and back and the remaining two with the bottom rails. Be sure to protect the stock with wood pads. As soon as you have tightened all the clamps, use a tape measure to check the safe for square *(above)*, measuring the distance between opposite corners; the two measurements should be equal. If not, install another bar clamp across the longer of the two diagonals, setting the clamp jaws on those already in place. Tighten the clamp a little at a time, measuring as you go until the two diagonals are equal.

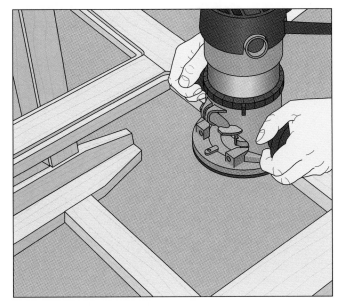

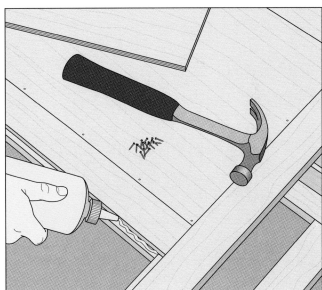

3 Installing the back panels

Set the safe down with its back facing up, then install a piloted ⅜-inch rabbeting bit in a router and adjust the cutting depth to ¹⁄₁₆ inch more than the thickness of the back panels you are using. Rout the rabbets around the inside edges of the back panel openings, keeping the bit's pilot bearing pressed against the stock throughout the cut *(above, left)*, then square the corners with a chisel. Cut two pieces of plywood to fit snugly into the openings and apply a thin bead of adhesive along the rabbets *(above, right)* and on the contacting surfaces of the plywood. Spread the glue evenly, set the panels in position, then use small finishing nails to secure them at 6- to 8-inch intervals.

INSTALLING COCKBEADING

1 Preparing the safe for cockbeading
Cut a rabbet around the inside edge of the front frame of the safe, using the same procedure you followed for the back panels *(page 99)*. This time, install a ¼-inch piloted rabbeting bit in your router and adjust the cutting depth to about ¼ inch. Keep the bit's pilot bearing butted against the stock as you make the cut *(right)*, then square the corners with a chisel.

Auxiliary fence

Featherboard

Shim

2 Milling the cockbeading
Make enough cockbeading from ¼-thick-stock to fit the rabbets cut in step 1, shaping it with molding cutters on a table saw. (Do not use narrow stock; instead, cut pieces that are at least 4 inches wide and then rip the cockbeading from them.) Install an auxiliary fence and raise the molding head into the wood fence to notch it. Use a featherboard to secure the workpiece; screw it to a shim so the pressure will be applied against the middle of the stock. To adjust the cut, center an edge of the board over a cutter, then butt the fence against the face of the stock. Hold the workpiece flush against the fence and the table as you feed it into the cutters *(left)*. Shape the opposite edge of the board the same way. Once all your stock has been milled, install a rip blade on the saw and cut the cockbeading from the boards, making it wide enough to protrude by ¼ inch from the rabbets in the safe.

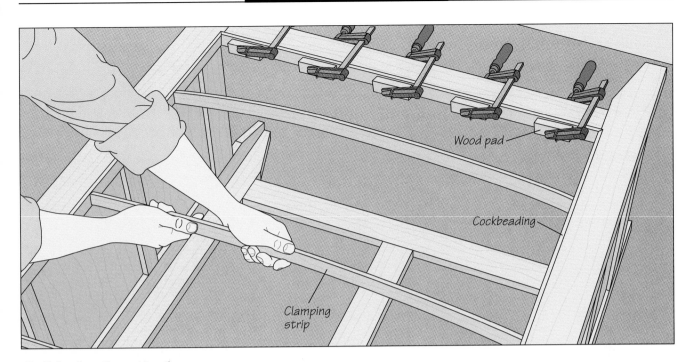

3 Gluing down the cockbeading
Cut the cockbeading to fit inside the front frame, mitering the ends. Cut and fit one piece at a time, aligning the mitered ends with the corners of the rabbets. Spread a little glue on the contacting surfaces. Use any suitable clamp to secure the cockbeading along the top and bottom of the opening, protecting the stock with wood pads; for the sides, wedge thin wood strips slightly longer than the gap between the cockbeading (above).

FASTENING THE TOP PANEL

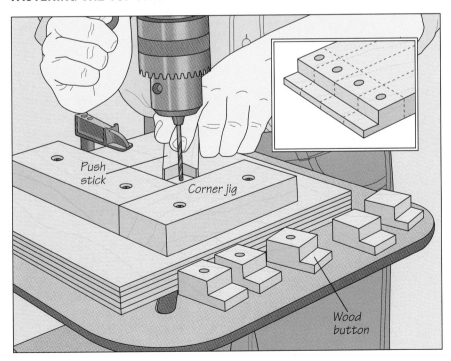

1 Making the wood buttons
If you are using wood buttons to install the top on the pie safe, you will need to make enough buttons to space them every 6 inches along the ends and edges of the panel. You can mass-produce the buttons from a single board of a thickness equal to the gap between the top edge of the top frame rails and the grooves you cut in the rails (page 93), less $\frac{1}{16}$ inch. Cut a $\frac{3}{8}$-inch rabbet at each end of the board, then rip it into 1-inch-wide strips and cut off the buttons about $1\frac{1}{2}$ inches from the ends (inset). To make screw holes in the buttons, install a $\frac{3}{16}$-inch bit in your drill press and fashion a corner jig from $\frac{3}{4}$-inch plywood and L-shaped support brackets. Clamp the jig to the machine table and steady the buttons with a push stick. Drill through the center of the unrabbeted portion of each button (left).

2 Installing the top

Set the top panel face down on the shop floor and position the safe upside down on top of it. Align the back of the cabinet with the back edge of the top and center the safe between the panel edges. Starting near the corners, fit the rabbeted ends of the wood buttons into the grooves in the top rails; space the buttons about 6 inches apart and leave a ⅛-inch gap between the bottom of the grooves and the lipped ends of the buttons to allow for wood movement. Drive screws to fasten the buttons in place *(right)*.

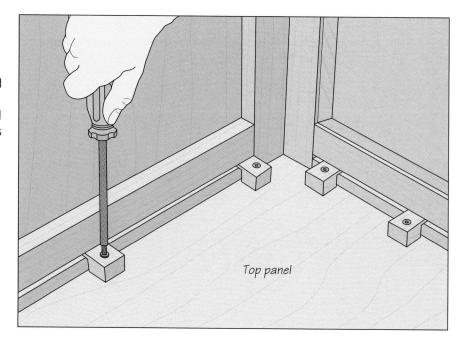

Top panel

INSTALLING CROWN MOLDING

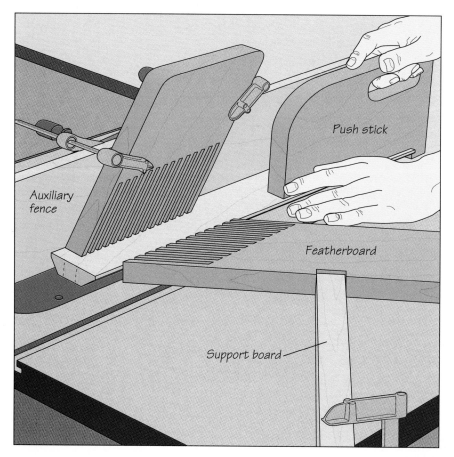

Auxiliary fence

Push stick

Featherboard

Support board

1 Cutting the molding

Fit a molding head with bevel cutters and mount the head on your table saw. Install and notch an auxiliary wood fence *(page 100)*, and position the fence for the desired profile. Secure the stock you will use to make the molding with two featherboards, clamping one to the fence above the blade, and a second to the saw table. Clamp a support board at a 90° angle to the second featherboard. Raise the cutters ⅛ inch above the table; do not make a full-depth cut in one pass. Press the stock against the fence as you slowly feed it into the cutters; finish the cut with a push stick. Reverse the board and repeat the cut on the other edge *(left)*. Make as many passes as necessary, raising the cutters ⅛ inch at a time, until you have reached the desired depth of cut. Install a rip blade on the saw and cut the molding from both sides of the workpiece, as represented by the dotted lines in the illustration.

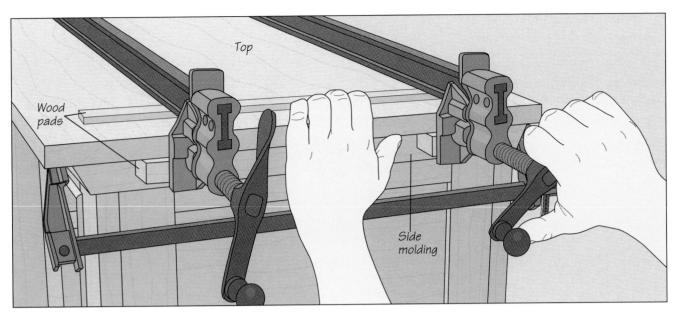

2 Installing the side molding

Fasten one side molding first, then the front piece, and finally the remaining side piece. Cut the molding pieces to length, mitering their ends. Spread some glue on the contacting surfaces between the first side piece and the top rail of the side and set the piece in position. To allow for wood movement, do not apply any glue between the molding and the top of the safe. Clamp the front piece to the front rail—without glue—to help you align the side piece properly. Install two bar clamps along the top to secure the side piece in place, tightening the clamps gradually until a thin bead of glue squeezes out from the joint; use wood pads to protect both the molding and the top (above).

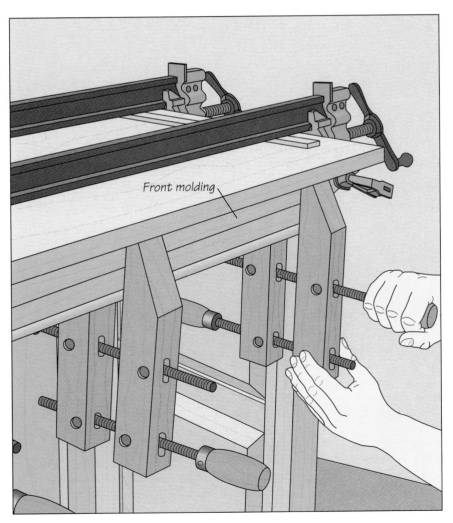

3 Installing the front molding

Once the side molding has been secured, remove the clamps holding the front piece in place and apply glue to it and to the front rail of the pie safe. Also spread some adhesive on the mitered ends of the molding. Use handscrews to clamp the front molding to the cabinet, spacing the clamps about 6 inches apart *(left)*. Finally, install the remaining side piece as you did the first one.

Adjustable shelving would no doubt have appealed to Shaker furniture makers. The feature gives a cabinet flexibility, adapting to changing needs and enabling the user to organize space most efficiently. The shelves can be held in place with shelf supports that fit in holes drilled in the stiles, as shown at right. Another option is shop-made wooden corner strips *(below)*, which are dadoed and attached to the interior corners of the pie safe to hold up the shelving.

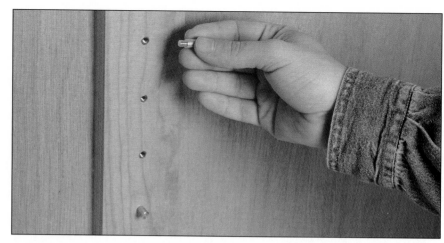

A metal shelf support pin is being screwed into a threaded sleeve in a pie safe stile. Inserted into drilled holes at evenly spaced intervals from the bottom to the top of the cabinet, the sleeves allow the pins— and shelves—to be installed at virtually any height inside the safe.

USING CORNER STRIPS

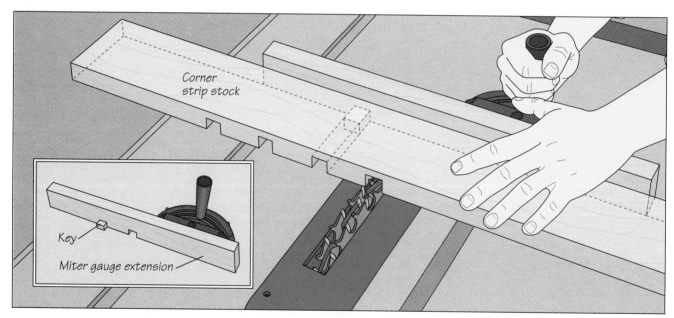

Corner strip stock

Key

Miter gauge extension

1 Making the corner strips

You can make four strips, one for each corner of the pie safe, from a single 4-inch-wide board that is long enough to extend from top to bottom of the cabinet. Install a dado head on your table saw and set the width equal to the thickness of the shelf supports you will use. Determine the desired spacing of the notches—typically about 2 inches—and cut two dadoes that distance apart in a miter gauge extension board. Align the left-hand dado with the blades and screw the extension to the gauge with the other dado offset to the right. Cut a 2-inch piece of shelf support stock and fit it into that dado, where it will serve as an indexing key *(inset)*. Cut your first dado about 8 inches from one end—or at whatever height you want your lowest shelf. Cut the second and subsequent dadoes by moving the piece to the right and fitting the previous dado over the key *(above)*. When the dadoes are all cut, rip the board into four 1-inch-wide corner strips.

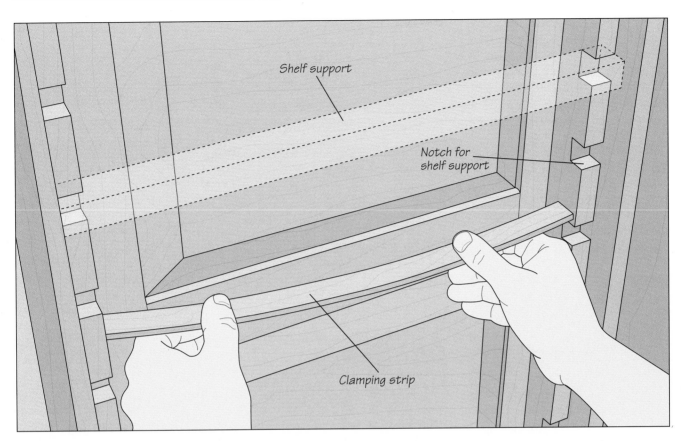

Shelf support

Notch for
shelf support

Clamping strip

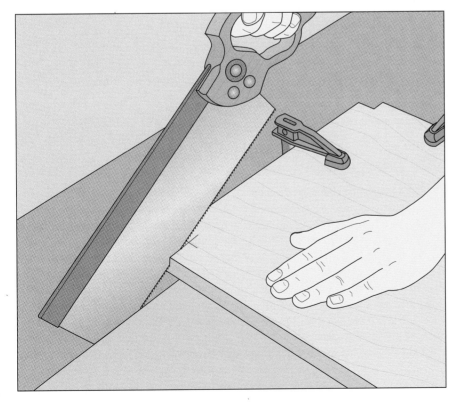

2 Installing the corner strips and shelf supports

Spread some glue on the contacting surfaces between the corner strips and the stiles of the pie safe, and position each strip, making sure that the dadoes face the interior of the cabinet. To clamp the strips in place, use thin wood scraps slightly longer than the gap between the strips *(above)*. For the shelf supports (represented by dotted lines in the illustration), measure the distance between the front and back stiles of the safe and cut the pieces to fit. Ensure that the supports are wide enough to hold the shelves securely.

3 Preparing the shelves

All four corners of each shelf must be notched to fit around the corner strips. Measure and mark each shelf, clamp it face down to a work surface, and cut out the corners with a backsaw *(left)*.

TIN-PANEL DOORS

The doors of the pie safe are joined with the open version of the mortise-and-tenon joint used to assemble the cabinet. The reinforcing pegs will prevent the joints from racking, even under the heaviest use. As shown below, you can make the joint on your table saw with a shop-made jig. Once the doors are assembled, they are rabbeted to accept the tin panels *(page 108)*. As shown on page 111, a variety of special punches are available for piercing the panels themselves. Once the panels are installed, the doors can be mounted to the safe with simple butt hinges *(page 114)*.

The doors of the pie safe are assembled with mortise-and-tenons, reinforced by wood pegs. The tin panels sit in rabbets along the inside edges of the doors and are held in place by strips of molding.

MAKING THE DOORS

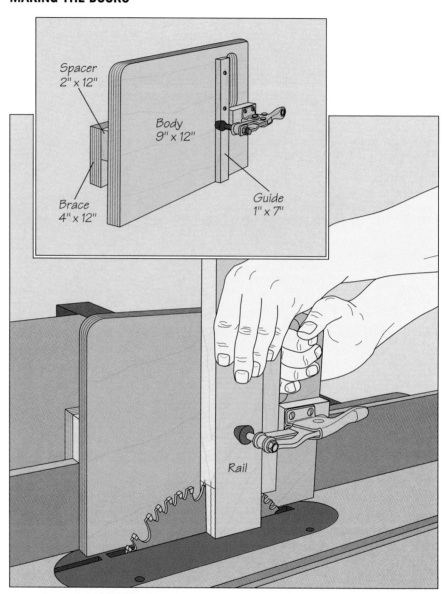

1 Cutting the tenon cheeks in the rails

Cut open mortise-and-tenons on your table saw using the shop-made jig shown in the inset. Refer to the dimensions suggested, making sure the thickness of the spacer and width of the brace enable the jig to slide along the rip fence without wobbling. Cut the body and brace from ¾-inch plywood and the guide and spacer from solid wood. Saw an oval hole for a handle in the jig body and attach the guide to the body in front of the handle. Screw a wood block to the body below the handle and attach a toggle clamp to the block. Finally, fasten the spacer and brace in place. To cut the tenon cheeks in the door rails, butt the workpiece against the guide and clamp it in place. Set the cutting height to the tenon length, position the fence to align one of the cutting marks on the rail with the blade and slide the jig along the fence to make the cut *(above)*. Turn the rail around to cut the other cheek, then repeat the cuts at the other end of the rail and at both ends of the remaining rails.

2 Cutting the tenon shoulders

Screw a board to the miter gauge as an extension. Then, holding one of the door rails against the extension, adjust the blade height to the depth of the tenon shoulder. Align the shoulder with the blade, butt a notched stop block against the stock, and clamp the block to the extension; the notch in the stop block will prevent sawdust from accumulating between it and the workpiece. Holding the rail flush against the extension and the stop block, feed the stock with the miter gauge to cut the first shoulder. To saw the opposite shoulder, turn the rail over *(right)*. Repeat to cut the tenon shoulders at the other end of the rail and in the remaining rails. **(Caution: Blade guard removed for clarity.)**

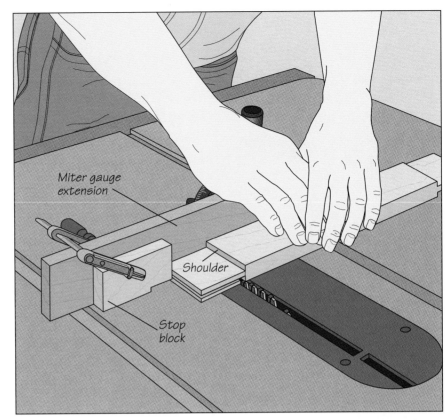

3 Cutting the mortises in the stiles

Use the tenoning jig to saw the mortises in the door stiles. Outline the mortises on the ends of the stiles, using a completed tenon as a guide. Then clamp one of the stiles to the jig, reset the blade height to the tenon length, and position the fence to align one of the cutting marks with the blade. Slide the jig along the fence to cut one side of the mortise, then turn the stile around to cut the other side *(left)*. Reposition the fence and make as many passes as necessary to clear out the waste between the kerfs. Repeat the cuts at the other end of the stile and at both ends of the remaining stiles.

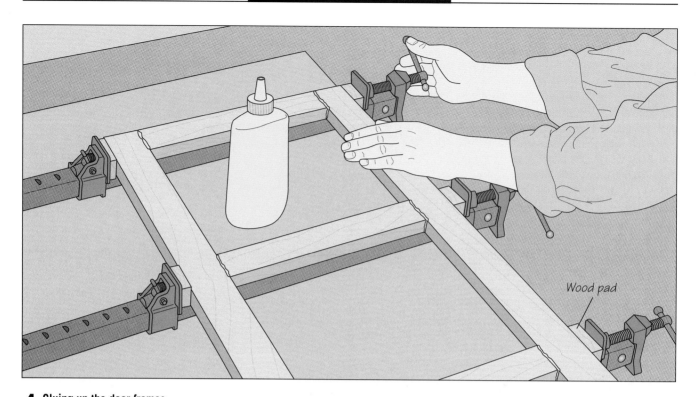

Wood pad

4 Gluing up the door frames
Dry-fit the rails and stiles of the doors and use a chisel, if necessary, to fine-tune any ill-fitting joints. Spread glue on the contacting surfaces of the mortises and tenons, then use bar clamps to secure the joints, aligning the bars with the rails. Use wood pads to protect the stock and tighten the clamps until a little glue squeezes out of the joints *(above)*.

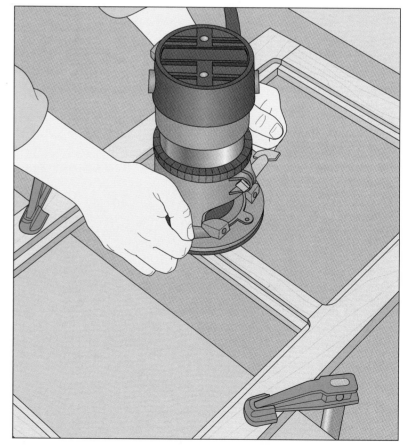

5 Preparing the door frames for panels
Once the adhesive has cured, remove the clamps and secure the frames inside-face up on a work surface. To cut the rabbets in the frames for the tin panels, install a piloted 3/8-inch rabbeting bit in a router. Although your final depth will equal the combined thickness of the panels and the molding you will be installing—typically 5/8 inch—adjust the bit to cut the rabbets in two or more passes. Rout the rabbets moving clockwise around the inside edges of the panel openings, keeping the bit's pilot bearing pressed against the stock throughout each cut *(right)*. Once you reach your final depth, square the corners of the rabbets with a chisel.

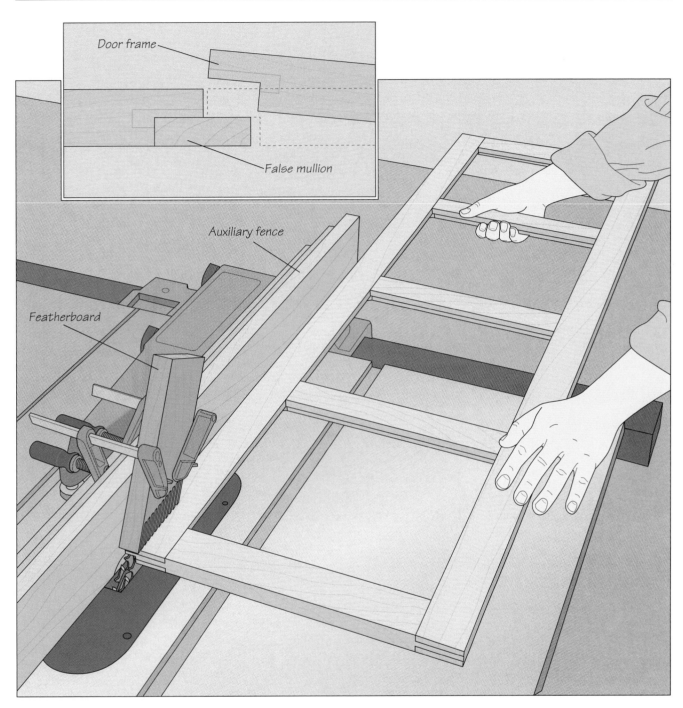

Door frame

False mullion

Auxiliary fence

Featherboard

6 Preparing the door frames for the false mullion

To enable the pie safe doors to close properly, cut a rabbet along the inside face of both doors at their contacting edges; a wood strip, known as a false mullion, will be glued into the rabbet of the left-hand door so the doors will rest flush when closed *(page 115)*. The 1/8-inch gap between the right-hand door and the edge of the mullion will prevent the doors from binding when they are closed, as shown in the end-on view in the inset. For the rab-

bets, install a dado head on your table saw and adjust its width to 1/2 inch and its height to 5/16 inch. Attach an auxiliary fence to your table saw rip fence, position the fence for the cutting width, and notch the wooden fence with the blades. To support the door frames, clamp a featherboard to the fence above the dado head. Feed each frame inside-face down with both hands *(above)*, keeping it flat on the table and pressed flush against the fence.

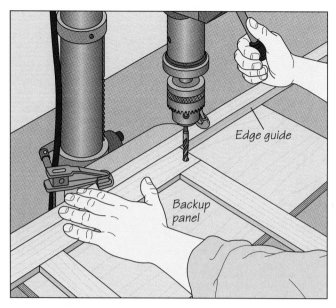

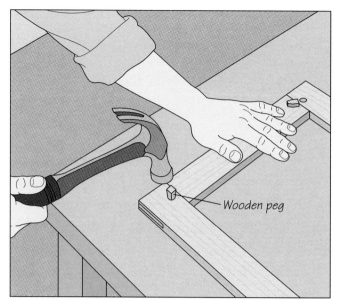

7 Pegging the mortise-and-tenons

Mark peg holes at all four corners of each door frame, centering them on the front face of the rails 1½ inches from the side edge of the door. Install a ⁵/₁₆-inch brad-point bit in your drill press, place a backup panel on the machine table to minimize tearout, and set one of the door frames on top, centering a drilling mark under the bit. Adjust the drilling depth to about two-thirds the thickness of the frame. Butt a board against the frame and clamp it in place as an edge guide. Then, holding the frame against the guide, drill the hole *(above, left)*. Bore the remaining holes in both frames the same way. Cut a peg for each hole from a piece of solid stock, making it slightly shorter than the depth of the holes. The pegs should be cut square, tapered at the bottom end and with a slight chamfer at the top. Tap each peg into its hole with a hammer *(above, right)*, letting it protrude about ¹/₁₆ inch.

MAKING THE TIN PANELS

1 Securing the pattern to the panel

Tin panels and the tools used to punch holes in them are available from folk-art supply houses. The best way to punch the holes in the panels so they are all the same is to use a pattern as a template. Several common patterns are illustrated on page 111; use a photocopier with an enlargement feature to produce a version of the desired pattern that is the same size as your panels. Then set one of the panels inside-face up on a backup board, center the pattern on the panel, and fix the paper to the tin with masking tape. To secure the panel to the backup board, use push pins, tapping them into the board every few inches around the perimeter of the panel.

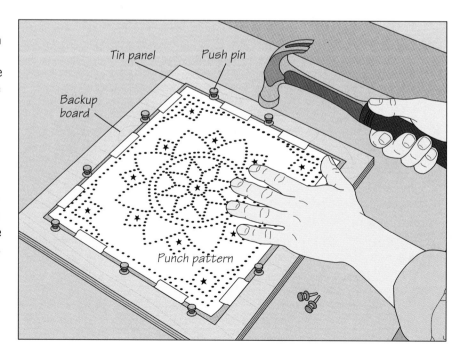

TRADITIONAL TIN PANEL PATTERNS

COMMON TIN PUNCH TOOLS AND THE CUTS THEY MAKE

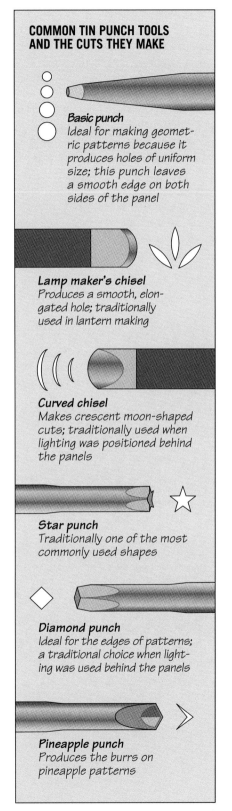

Basic punch
Ideal for making geometric patterns because it produces holes of uniform size; this punch leaves a smooth edge on both sides of the panel

Lamp maker's chisel
Produces a smooth, elongated hole; traditionally used in lantern making

Curved chisel
Makes crescent moon-shaped cuts; traditionally used when lighting was positioned behind the panels

Star punch
Traditionally one of the most commonly used shapes

Diamond punch
Ideal for the edges of patterns; a traditional choice when lighting was used behind the panels

Pineapple punch
Produces the burrs on pineapple patterns

Courtesy of Country Accents, Montoursville, PA

2 Punching the holes

Use a hammer and the appropriate punch or chisel for the type of hole you wish to produce. Holding the punch vertically on one of the pattern holes, strike the tool with the hammer *(right)*. A minimum amount of force is needed to puncture the panel; the harder you strike the punch, the larger the hole will be. Punch all the holes the same way, changing to a different punch or chisel as necessary. If you are using a metal other than tin for the panels, such as mild steel, you will need to file the sharp edges of the holes on the outside face of the panels. With tin, filing is not necessary.

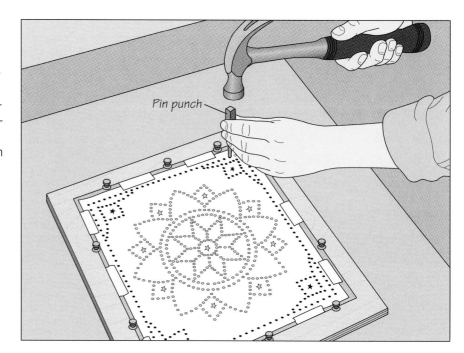

Pin punch

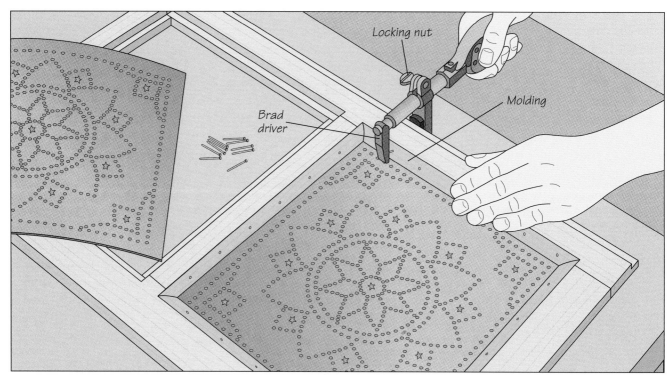

Locking nut

Molding

Brad driver

3 Installing the tin panels and molding

Make four strips of molding for each panel as you would for the glass doors of a wall clock *(page 125)*. Then set the door frames outside-face down on a work surface and place a panel and molding in position. The sharp edges of the punched holes should be facing down. Bore pilot holes for finishing nails through the molding and into the frame every 2 inches, then drive the nails using a brad driver. To use the driver, insert a nail into a pilot hole, then position the jaws and tighten the locking nut. Holding the frame steady, squeeze the jaws to set the nail *(above)*.

INSTALLING THE DOORS

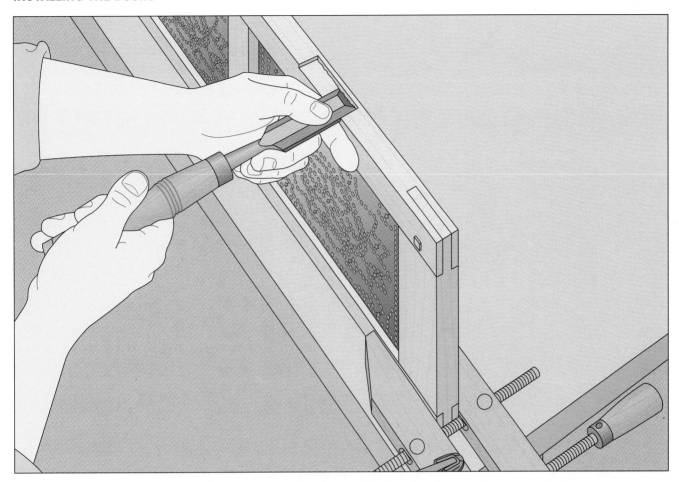

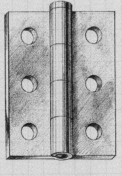

SHOP TIP

Making butterfly hinges
With their wing-shaped
leaves, butterfly hinges
were commonly used on
Shaker furniture. Today,
they are expensive and
difficult to find. However,
transforming a standard
butt hinge into a butterfly
hinge is a simple matter.
Grind the tops and bottoms of butt hinge leaves
on your bench grinder until you cut away enough
metal to produce the characteristic shape.

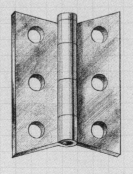

1 Installing the hinges on the doors
Secure one of the doors hinge-edge
up in a bench vise. Outline one hinge
leaf about 6 inches from the top of the
door and another 6 inches from the bottom. Then, holding a chisel vertically,
score the outline and cut it slightly deeper than the thickness of the hinge leaf.
Hold the chisel bevel up to pare the
waste from the mortise *(above)*. Once
you have cleared out the remaining
mortises on both doors, set the hinges
in their mortises, drill pilot holes, and
screw them in place.

Paper spacers

2 **Installing the hinges on the safe**
Position one of the doors in the cabinet, slipping two or three sheets of paper under the door as spacers. Use a bar clamp to hold the door in place, then mark the tops and bottoms of the hinge leaves on the inside edge of the front frame stiles *(above)*. Remove the door, slip the pins out of the hinges, and outline the free hinge leaves on the safe, using the marks you made to determine the height of the outlines. Make sure the hinge pins will protrude far enough from the safe so as not to bind against the cockbeading when the door is opened and closed. Chisel out the hinge mortises on the cabinet stiles as you did on the doors *(page 113)* and screw the hinge leaves in place. Repeat the process with the other door.

3 **Hanging the door**
Once all the hinge leaves are installed, it is time to hang the door. Lift one of the doors into position so the hinge leaves on the door and the safe engage *(above)*. Slip each hinge pin in place to join the leaves. Hang the other door the same way.

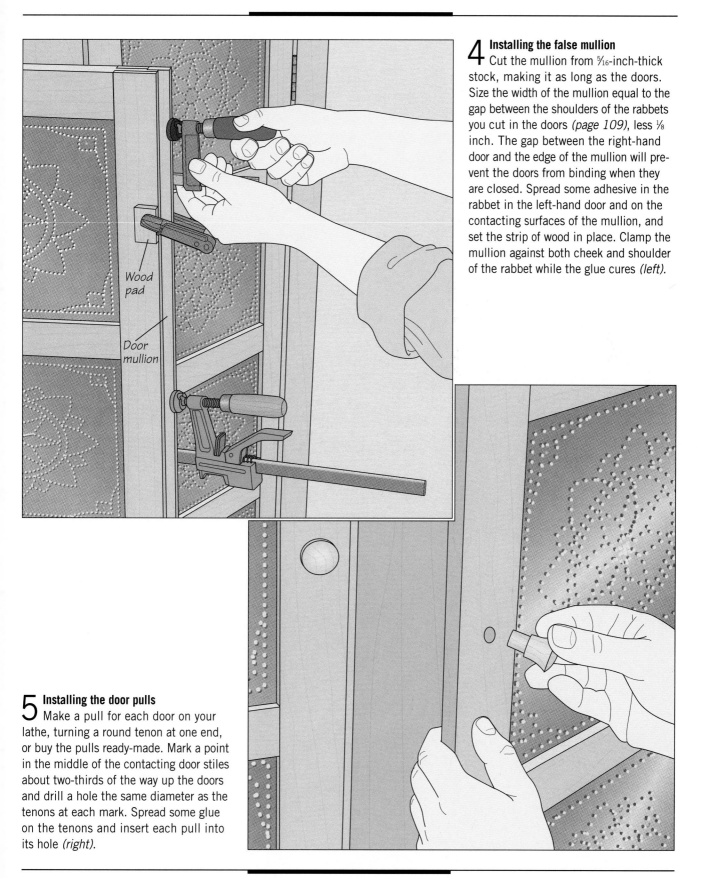

4 Installing the false mullion
Cut the mullion from 5/16-inch-thick stock, making it as long as the doors. Size the width of the mullion equal to the gap between the shoulders of the rabbets you cut in the doors *(page 109)*, less 1/8 inch. The gap between the right-hand door and the edge of the mullion will prevent the doors from binding when they are closed. Spread some adhesive in the rabbet in the left-hand door and on the contacting surfaces of the mullion, and set the strip of wood in place. Clamp the mullion against both cheek and shoulder of the rabbet while the glue cures *(left)*.

Wood pad

Door mullion

5 Installing the door pulls
Make a pull for each door on your lathe, turning a round tenon at one end, or buy the pulls ready-made. Mark a point in the middle of the contacting door stiles about two-thirds of the way up the doors and drill a hole the same diameter as the tenons at each mark. Spread some glue on the tenons and insert each pull into its hole *(right)*.

SHAKER CLASSICS

Made from quartersawn cherry veneer, the band for the box shown above is bent around a drying form after first being soaked in hot water and softened. The band is secured in its bent shape by copper tacks.

The same principles that guided the Shakers in their daily lives—purity, wholesomeness, and usefulness—are reflected in everything they built. Each of the small Shaker projects featured in this chapter—a wall clock, a step stool, an oval box, and a pegboard—is a classic example of this single-minded philosophy.

To the Shakers, no household item, no matter how small, could be considered frivolous or simple adornment. The term "knickknack" had no place in their lexicon. Whatever they made had to be strong, durable, and without fault. It also had to be perfectly suited to the purpose for which it was designed.

Wall clocks, like the one shown on page 118, and tall, freestanding grandfather clocks were essential to the Shakers' disciplined lives, but the Shakers designed other types for special needs. The homely "wag-on-the-wall" clock had no case, but only a small frame to protect the mechanism, and simply hung from a peg. They also made basic clocks for their barns that had only an hour hand. Even less ornate was the "tower clock" at Sabbathday Lake, Maine. This timepiece had no face or hands at all. Its main feature was an 80-pound brass engine bell that sounded loudly on the hour.

Oval boxes, like those shown at left, were used to store a variety of dry goods. With their distinctive swallowtail fingers, straight sides, and smooth finish, the boxes were elevated by Shaker craftsmanship from mere vessels into things of beauty. That the Shakers made these boxes by the thousands while holding to a high standard of excellence is remarkable—and typical of their creed and craftsmanship.

The tall cabinets built by the Shakers created the need to access high shelves. The step stool shown on page 129 answered this requirement, becoming a mobile but sturdy staircase. Although its treads were often dovetailed into the sides, strength, rather than appearance, justified the attractive joinery.

The pegboard *(page 138)* is an example of how the Shakers stretched the usefulness of a humble item until it became an indispensable part of their lives. Pegs lined the walls of most Shaker homes, hanging everything from bookshelves and kitchen implements to clocks and chairs.

The rails, stiles, and divider of the frame for a Shaker wall clock are being glued up, secured by bar clamps. The rails and stiles shown at left are joined with rabbets, while the divider simply fits into dadoes cut across the stiles.

WALL CLOCK

The Shakers led very disciplined, structured lives. They rose at 4:00 a.m. in the summer, allowing themselves to sleep in an hour later in winter. They stopped working at 7:30 p.m. on summer evenings and at 8:00 p.m. in the winter, one-half hour before evening worship. They also ate their meals at precise times. A Shaker elder from Ohio once said, "The clock is an emblem of the Shaker community because everything goes on time. Promptness, absolute punctuality, is a *sine qua non* of a successful community."

In the early, lean years of their movement, Shaker communities considered themselves fortunate to own one working "alarum" clock. As the sect prospered, and as clock makers joined the movement, the availability of the timepieces spread. The Shakers never carried pocket watches, however. These were considered unnecessary indulgences.

The mechanisms of original Shaker clocks were made from brass or wood. A less costly and more reliable modern alternative is to buy a quartz clock movement. These can be ordered complete with metal dial and with or without a pendulum from many hobby supply stores. The following pages show how to assemble a case for a Shaker-style wall clock.

Isaac Newton Youngs was one of the few Shaker clock makers to design and construct cases to house his timepieces. The clock shown below was inspired by one that he built in the spring of 1840 at the New Lebanon community in New York State.

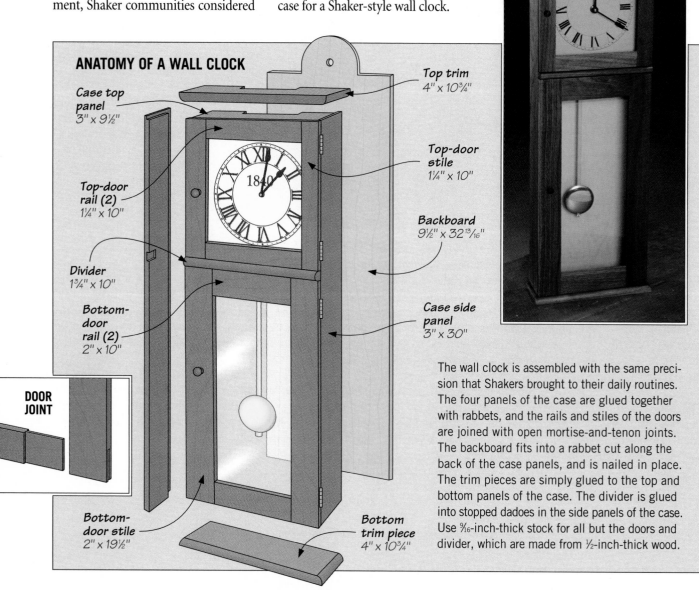

ANATOMY OF A WALL CLOCK

Case top panel
3" x 9½"

Top trim
4" x 10¾"

Top-door stile
1¼" x 10"

Top-door rail (2)
1¼" x 10"

Backboard
9½" x 32¹³/₁₆"

Divider
1¾" x 10"

Bottom-door rail (2)
2" x 10"

Case side panel
3" x 30"

DOOR JOINT

Bottom-door stile
2" x 19½"

Bottom trim piece
4" x 10¾"

The wall clock is assembled with the same precision that Shakers brought to their daily routines. The four panels of the case are glued together with rabbets, and the rails and stiles of the doors are joined with open mortise-and-tenon joints. The backboard fits into a rabbet cut along the back of the case panels, and is nailed in place. The trim pieces are simply glued to the top and bottom panels of the case. The divider is glued into stopped dadoes in the side panels of the case. Use ⁹/₁₆-inch-thick stock for all but the doors and divider, which are made from ½-inch-thick wood.

BUILDING THE CASE

1 Rabbeting the side panels

Prepare the case pieces for assembly by rabbeting the ends of the side panels on your table saw. Install a dado head on the saw and adjust its width to $\frac{5}{16}$ inch. Set the cutting height at $\frac{5}{16}$ inch. Screw a wooden auxiliary fence to the rip fence and notch it with the dado head. To help you feed the long stock across the saw table and to minimize tearout, screw a board as an extension to the miter gauge. Then, butting one side panel against the fence and the extension, feed it along with the miter gauge to cut the first rabbet *(right)*. Repeat at the other end of the board and at both ends of the second side panel. To prepare the side panels for the backboard, cut a rabbet along the back edge of each board.

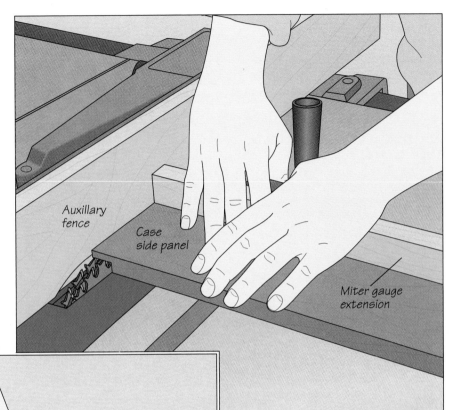

Auxillary fence

Case side panel

Miter gauge extension

2 Preparing the side panels for the divider

Outline the dado on the front edge of each side panel that will accept the divider. The length of the dado should be about one-half the width of the divider. Install a straight bit the same diameter as the dado width in a router, butt one side panel on a work surface against a backup board, and align the bit over the outline. Butt a board as an edge guide against the router base plate and clamp the setup in place. With the base plate flush against the edge guide, plunge the bit into the backup board and guide it into the side panel, stopping the cut at your end line *(left)*. Rout the dado in the second side panel, then square both dadoes with a chisel.

Backup board

Side panel

Dado end line

Edge guide

3 Preparing the divider for installation

Leaving the auxiliary fence and miter gauge extension on your table saw, notch the ends of the divider to fit into the dadoes you cut in the side panels. Position the fence to cut a ⁵⁄₁₆-inch-wide notch and set the cutting height of the dado head to ⅞ inch. Holding the divider on edge and flush against the fence and extension, feed the miter gauge into the blades. Turn the board around and notch the other end *(right)*.

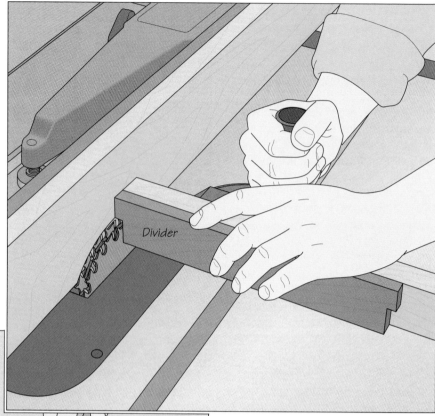

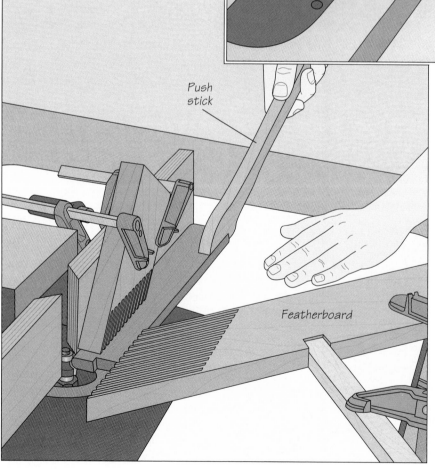

4 Rounding over the divider

Round over the front edge of the divider on a router table. Install a piloted ¼-inch round-over bit in a router, mount the tool in a table, and align the fence with the bit's pilot bearing. To support the divider, use three featherboards, clamping two to the fence, one on each side of the bit, and one to the table. Brace this second featherboard with a support board secured to the table. (Note: The featherboard on the outfeed side of the fence has been removed for clarity.) Now use a push stick to feed the divider across the table *(left)*. Make two passes to round over each face of the stock, starting with a shallow cut and raising the bit slightly for the second pass.

5 Cutting the backboard

Use a piece of solid wood for the backboard—a Shaker builder would typically have used pine. To mark out the arch at the top of the backboard, first mark a centerline near the top end of the stock and use a compass to outline a circle with a radius of 2¼ inches in the middle of the stock, centered 2¼ inches from the top end. Next, mark a straight line across the stock 3⅜ inches from the top end. Draw two perpendicular lines as shown to accommodate the notches in the top panel. Use your band saw to cut out the arch. Set the stock on the saw table and feed the piece with both hands, making the straight cuts first and then sawing the semicircle *(left)*.

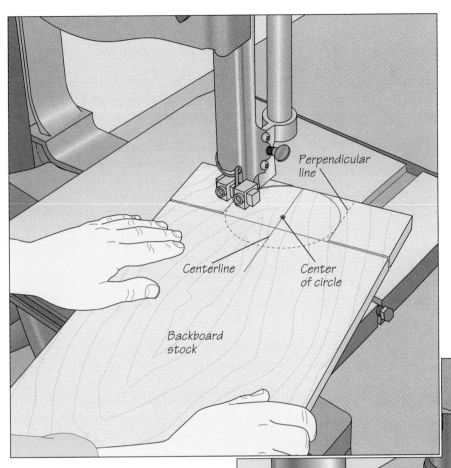

Perpendicular line

Centerline

Center of circle

Backboard stock

6 Drilling the peghole in the backboard

To ensure the clock will hang level, the peg hole must be centered between the edges of the backboard. Mark a drilling point on your centerline 1⅞ inches from the top of the arch, then bore the hole on your drill press. Install a ½-inch brad-point bit in the machine and clamp a backup panel to the table to help minimize tearout. Position your mark directly under the bit, clamp the backboard in place, and drill the hole *(right)*.

Backup panel

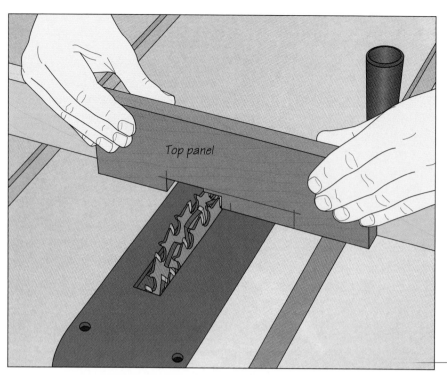

7 **Preparing the top panel and top trim piece for the backboard**

You will need to cut a notch in the back edge of the top panel and top trim piece of the clock case to accommodate the backboard. Outline the notch in the middle of the edge of each piece. Leave the dado head and miter gauge extension on your table saw, but move the fence out of the way. To cut the notches, align the dado head with one end of the outline, raise the blades to the thickness of the backboard, and use the miter gauge to feed the panel into the cut. Then, slide the workpiece along the extension by the width of the kerf and make another pass *(left)*, continuing until you reach the other end of the outline. Use the same setup to prepare the top trim piece for the backboard.

8 **Assembling the case**

Smooth the case pieces and the backboard, using progressively finer sandpaper, finishing with 220-grit. Assemble the case in two steps, starting with the four panels and the divider. Spread glue on all the contacting surfaces of the pieces and clamp the joints securely, as shown in the color photo on page 116. Check the corners for square by measuring the distance between diagonally opposite corners of the case. The two measurements should be the same; if not, adjust the clamping pressure until they are. Once the glue has cured, remove the clamps, set the assembly face down on a work surface, and fit the backboard in position. It is secured with nails; do not use any glue, since the board must be free to move as the wood swells and contracts with humidity changes. Bore pilot holes for finishing nails through the backboard and into the rabbets along the back edges of the case panels. Space the holes about 4 inches apart, then drive the nails in place *(right)*.

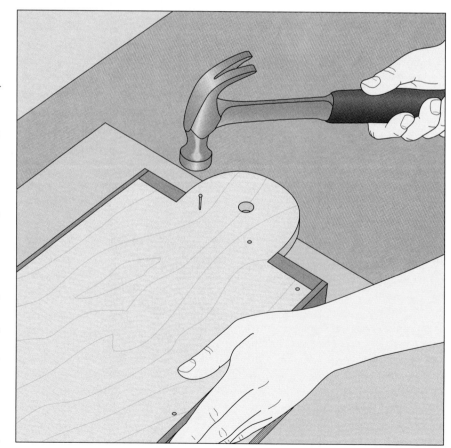

MAKING THE DOORS

1 Cutting the tenons in the rails

Use your table saw to cut the open mortise-and-tenons that join the rails and stiles of the doors. Saw the pieces to size, then install a commercial tenoning jig on the saw table; the model shown slides in the miter slot. Clamp one of the rails end-up to the jig, using a wood pad to protect the stock. Make the cutting height equal to the stock width and position the jig so the outside faces of the blade and the workpiece are aligned. Push the jig forward to feed the rail into the blade *(right)*, then turn the stock around and repeat the cut on the other edge. Move the jig toward the blade slightly so the thickness of the tenon will be equal to about one-third the stock thickness and make two more passes. Repeat the process to cut tenon cheeks on the other end of the rail and at both ends of the remaining rails.

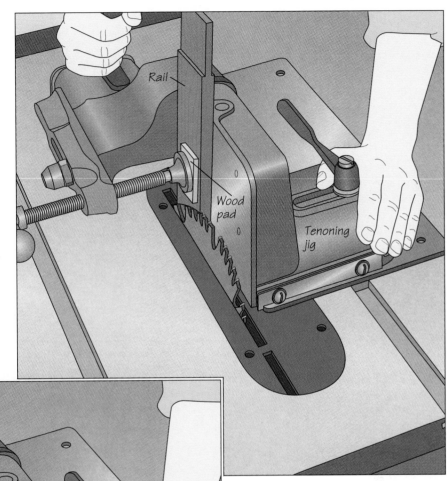

2 Sawing the mortises

Clamp one of the door stiles end-up to the jig, position the jig to center the edge of the workpiece with the blade, and feed the stock into the cut *(left)*. Then move the jig very slightly away from the blade to enlarge the mortise. Make another pass, turn the stile around in the jig, and feed it into the blade again. Next, test-fit one of the rail tenons in the mortise. If the fit is too tight, move the jig away from the blade slightly and make two more passes, continuing until the tenon fits snugly in the mortise. Use the same procedure to cut the mortises at the other end of the stile and at both ends of the remaining stiles. You can also use a shop-made jig to cut this joint, as shown on page 106.

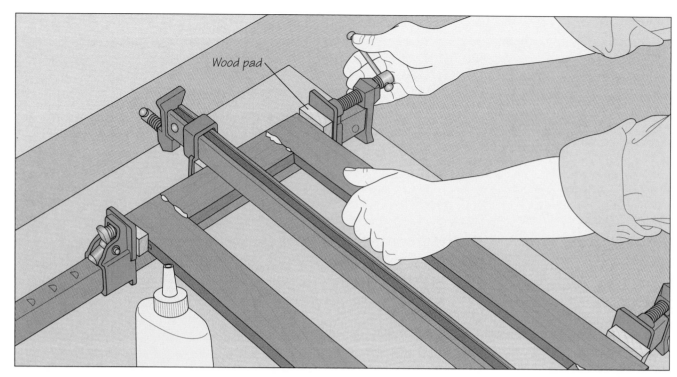

Wood pad

3 Gluing up the rails and stiles

Dry-assemble the two door frames to check the fit of the joints. If they are too tight, use a chisel to pare away excess wood; if any of the tenons extends beyond the outside edges of the stiles, sand it flush. Then spread glue on the contacting surfaces of the rail tenons and stile mortises, and assemble the frames. Use three clamps to secure each assembly, aligning one with each rail and centering a third between the stiles; protect the stock with wood pads. Tighten the clamps a little at a time until a thin glue bead squeezes out of the joints *(above)*, checking the frame for square as you go.

4 Preparing the door frames for glass panels

Each door will have a glass panel that sits in rabbets cut along the inside edges of the frame; the glass is held in place by strips of molding. Once the glue has cured, remove the clamps and cut the rabbets on a router table. Install a ½-inch top-piloted straight bit in a router and mount the tool in a table. Adjust the bit height to the combined thickness of the glass and molding you will be using. Remove the fence and set a door frame on the table. Turn on the tool and press the inside edge of the frame against the bit near one corner, then rotate the stock clockwise to cut the rabbets along the rails and stiles *(right)*. Keep the frame flat on the table as you feed it into the bit. Square the corners of the rabbets with a mallet and a wood chisel. Repeat the procedure for the other door.

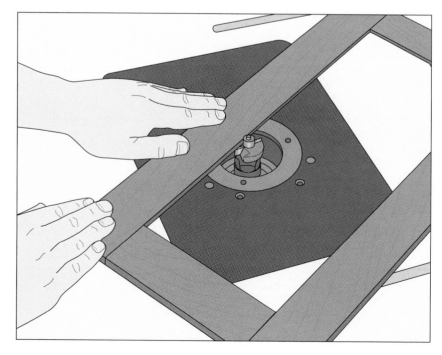

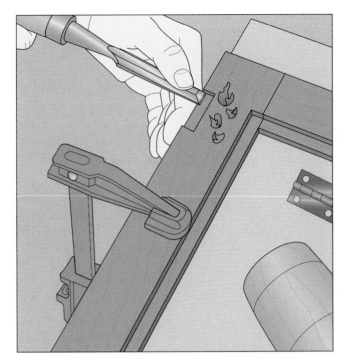

5 Mounting hinges on the doors

The doors are hung on the clock case with butt hinges; the hinge leaves are concealed in recesses cut into the inside faces of the doors and the front edges of the case. Position each door in turn on the case and outline the hinge leaves on the doors and the case. To cut the recesses in the doors, clamp the frame to a work surface inside-face up. Cut each recess with a chisel in two steps. Start by holding the chisel vertically on your outline with the bevel facing the waste and tap the handle with a mallet, moving the chisel along to score the entire outline. Then pare away the waste in thin layers, holding the chisel horizontally, bevel-side up *(left)*. Test-fit a hinge leaf in the recess periodically, stopping when the recess is about 1/64 inch deeper than the thickness of the leaf. With the hinge leaf in position, mark the screw holes in the recess, bore a pilot hole at each mark, and screw the hinge leaf to the door. Use the same procedure to cut the recesses in the front edges of the case.

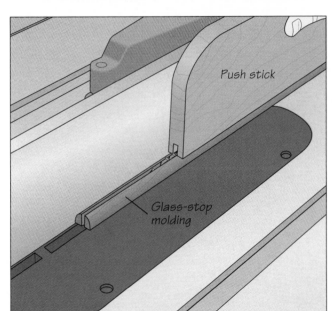

6 Making the glass-stop molding

Cut the molding that will secure the glass in the doors from a single 5/8-inch-thick board. Start by rounding over both edges of the piece as you did for the divider *(page 120)*, then rip the molding from the board on your table saw, feeding the stock with a push stick *(above)*. Saw the molding to fit into the rabbets in the doors, making 45° miter cuts at the ends of each piece. Cut and fit one piece at a time, making sure to align the miter cuts with the corners of the rabbets.

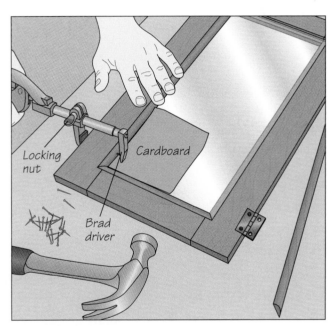

7 Securing the glass

Have glass panels prepared for the door, cutting them 1/8 inch shorter and narrower than their openings. This will leave a 1/16-inch gap around the glass to allow for wood movement. Apply your finish to the door frames, let it dry, then set the door frames and glass on a work surface and place the molding in position. Bore pilot holes for finishing nails through the molding and into the frame every 2 inches, then drive the nails using a brad driver. To use the driver, insert a nail into a pilot hole, then position the jaws and tighten the locking nut. Holding the frame steady, squeeze the jaws to set the nail *(above)*. Use a piece of cardboard to protect the glass.

FINAL ASSEMBLY

1 Gluing on the trim pieces
Cut the top and bottom trim pieces to size, then round over one face of their side and front edges on a router table using a 9½-inch round-over bit *(page 120)*. To install the pieces, set the clock case on its back on a work surface and spread glue on the contacting surfaces of the trim pieces and the top and bottom panels. Position the trim pieces so their back edges are flush with the back of the case and secure them with bar clamps spaced every 4 to 6 inches. Tighten the clamps *(right)* until a little glue squeezes out of the joints.

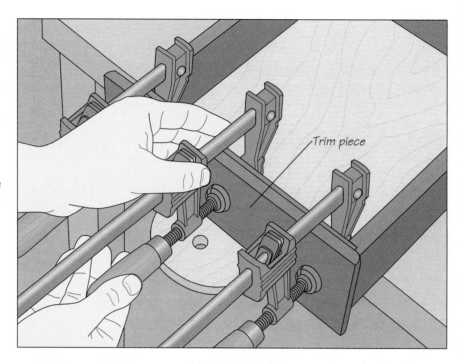

Trim piece

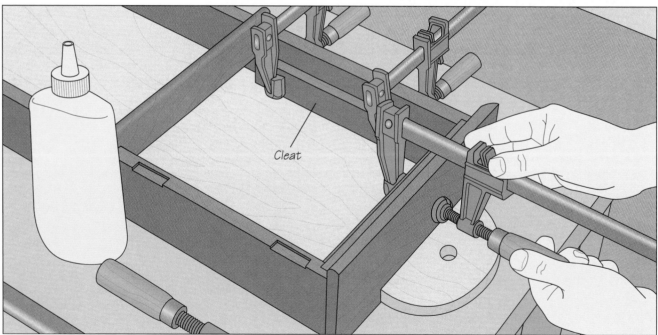

Cleat

2 Preparing the case for the dial and clock mechanism
The dial and clock mechanism are attached to a thin plywood backing board, which in turn is screwed to cleats glued to the inside of the case. Cut two cleats to fit along the inside face of the case side panels between the top panel and the divider. Cut a third one to run along the inside face of the top panel between the side panels. To help you mark the positions of the cleats, test-fit the clock in the case, remembering to allow for the doors. Once the cleat position is certain, spread glue on the contacting surfaces between the cleats and the case, and clamp the cleats in place *(above)*.

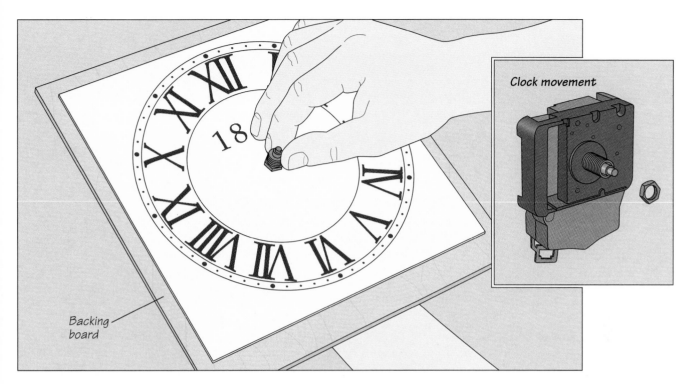

Clock movement

Backing
board

3 Assembling the clock mechanism

Assemble the clock mechanism following the manufacturer's directions. For the model shown, position the dial on the backing board provided and outline the shaft hole on the board. Remove the dial and bore the shaft hole through the backing board on your drill press. Fix the dial to the backing board with epoxy, making sure the dial is centered between the board's edges. To attach the clock movement *(inset)*, insert the shaft through the shaft hole and the dial, then tighten the nut on the shaft by hand *(above)*. If the shaft protrudes too far from the dial, loosen the nut, remove the movement and slip one or more washers between the movement and the backing board. A number of washers are supplied with most models.

4 Securing the clock assembly to the case

Position the backing board in the clock case and drill pilot holes for ¾-inch No. 6 wood screws through the board and into the cleats. Bore a hole at each corner, then drive in the screws *(left)*.

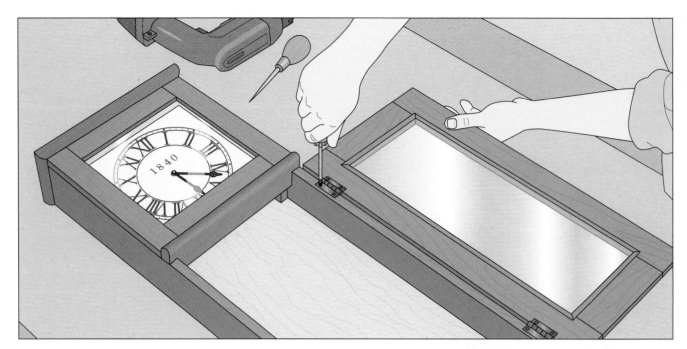

5 Hanging the doors

Set the clock on its back and position the top door on the case. With the hinge pin centered between the edges of the door and case, mark the hinge leaf screw holes in the case. Bore the holes and drive the screws, then repeat the process for the bottom door *(above)*. If either door binds against the divider, try sanding the binding rail. Now apply a finish to the clock case.

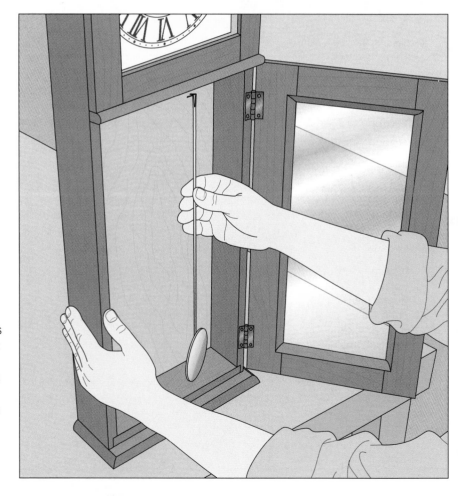

6 Installing the pendulum

Most pendulum weights have a brass finish that is easily scratched; the weight is usually protected by a plastic covering. Do not remove the covering until the pendulum has been mounted. Slide the pendulum rod under the clock face so its top end catches on the hook under the movement. The clock can now be hung on a wall from a hook or a Shaker pegboard like the one shown on page 138.

STEP STOOL

In their quest for order and efficiency, the Shakers built chests of drawers and cabinets that made good use of available space, often stretching from floor to ceiling. Step stools like the one shown below evolved to enable household members to gain access to the uppermost shelves. Depending on individual needs, the stools were made in two-, three-, and four-step versions. The taller stools often featured steadying rods screwed to the side to provide a hand hold.

Although these stools appeal to the modern eye, usefulness was the Shaker builder's sole concern. Through dovetails were chosen to attach the treads to the sides because the interlocking joints gave the stools strength and stability. Step-by-step instructions for cutting the joints by hand, much as a Shaker crafts-man might have done, are provided starting on page 130.

The stools were traditionally cut from ¾-inch-thick cherry, except for the ½-inch-thick crosspieces. Once you have cut your stock for the sides of the stool, use a pencil to mark the top, bottom, and front and back edges of each piece. This will help you avoid any confusion when you come to cut the pins at the sides' top ends.

ANATOMY OF A STEP STOOL

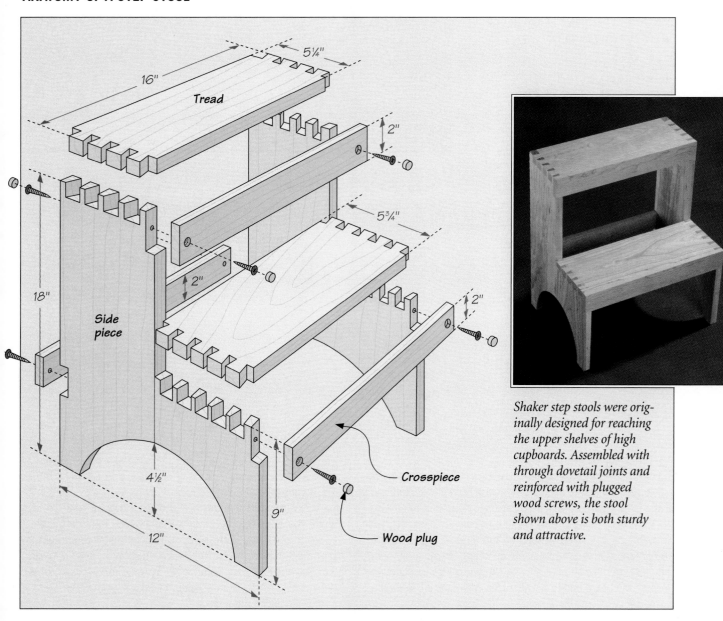

Shaker step stools were originally designed for reaching the upper shelves of high cupboards. Assembled with through dovetail joints and reinforced with plugged wood screws, the stool shown above is both sturdy and attractive.

CUTTING THE DOVETAILS

1 Notching the sides for the crosspieces

The sides are made from two boards glued together after the notches and the pins of the dovetail joint are cut in them. Outline the notches on the edges of each side piece, then cut them on your table saw. Install a dado head on the saw and set the cutting height to the notch width. Screw a board to the miter gauge as an extension. Make several passes to cut each notch *(right)*, feeding the stock up on edge with the miter gauge. Use the rip fence as a guide for cutting up to the notch end line.

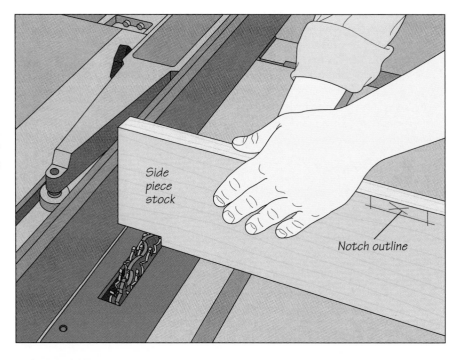

Side piece stock

Notch outline

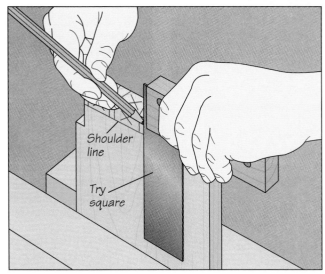

Shoulder line

Try square

2 Laying out the pins

Set a cutting gauge to the stock thickness and scribe a line around the top end of each side piece to mark the shoulder line of the tails. Next, use a dovetail square to outline the pins on the same end; the wide part of the pins should be on the inside face of the stock. Start with a half-pin at each edge and add evenly spaced pins in between. To complete the marking, secure the piece in a vise and use a try square and pencil to extend the lines on the board end to the shoulder lines *(above)*. Mark the waste sections with Xs as you go.

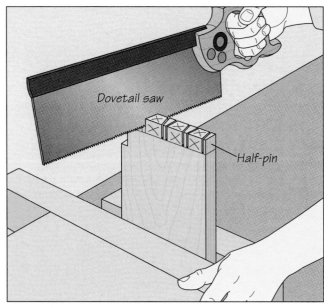

Dovetail saw

Half-pin

3 Cutting pins

Leave the piece in the vise and use a dovetail saw to cut along the edges of the pins, working from one side of the board to the other. For each cut, align the saw blade just to the waste side of the cutting line. Use smooth, even strokes, allowing the saw to cut on the push stroke *(above)*. Continue sawing right to the shoulder line, making sure that the blade is perpendicular to the line.

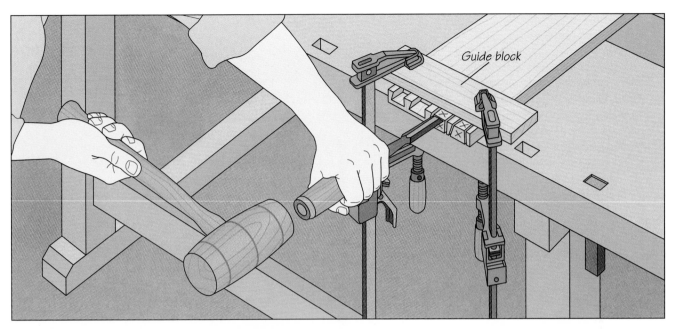

4 Chiseling out the waste

Set the side piece inside face up on a work surface and clamp on a guide block, aligning its edge with the shoulder line. Using a chisel no wider than the narrow side of the waste section, butt the flat side of the blade against the guide block. Hold the end of the chisel square to the face of the piece and strike it with a wooden mallet, scoring a line about ⅛ inch deep. Then turn the chisel toward the end of the panel about ⅛ inch below the surface of the wood and shave off a thin layer of waste *(above)*. Continue shaving away the waste in this fashion until you are about halfway through the thickness of the piece, then move on to the next section. When you have removed all the waste from this side, turn the piece over, and work from the other side *(left)* until the pins are completely exposed.

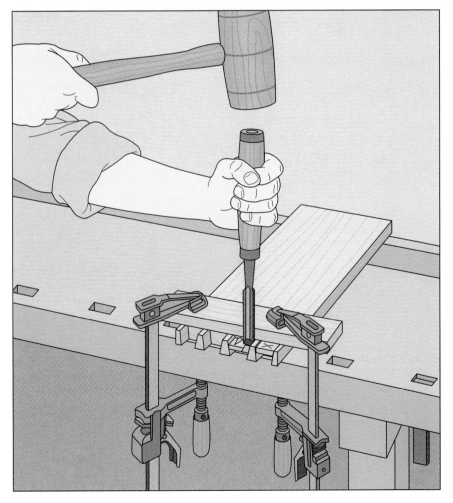

Although the Shakers did not have routers and commercial jigs at their disposal, the tools' efficacy for cutting dovetail joints quickly and precisely would certainly have appealed to them. The jig shown at right consists of two templates fastened to backup boards. The workpiece is secured to the jig and a stop block helps with positioning for repeat cuts. Here, a router fitted with a dovetail bit moves in and out of the slots of the tail board template.

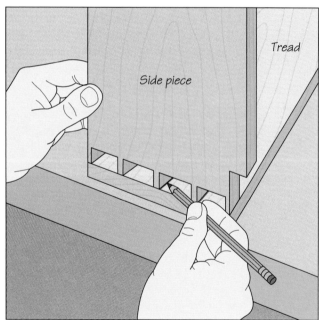

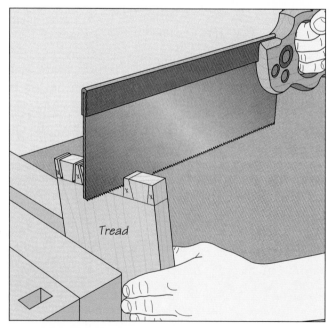

5 Laying out the tails

Set a tread bottom-face up on a work surface. Hold one of the side pieces pins down with its inside face aligned with the shoulder line of the tread. Use a pencil to outline the tails at each end of the tread *(above)*, then extend the lines on the board using a try square. Mark the waste with Xs and repeat the process with the remaining tread.

6 Cutting the tails and removing waste

Use a dovetail saw to cut the tails the same way you cut the pins *(step 2)*. Angling the board *(above)*, rather than the saw, makes for easier cutting. Saw smoothly and evenly, stopping just short of the shoulder line. You can also cut the tails on your band saw. Remove the waste with a chisel as in step 4.

7 **Testing the fit of the joints**
Before gluing up the stool, assemble it to check the fit of all the joints. Stand one of the side pieces on end, then align a tread with it. Press the joint together by hand as far as it will go *(right)*, then use a mallet to tap the tread the rest of the way into place. The boards should fit snugly, requiring only a light tapping; avoid using excessive force. If any joint is clearly too tight, mark the spot where it binds, then disassemble the boards and use a chisel to pare away a little more wood. Test-fit the joint again and adjust it further, as necessary.

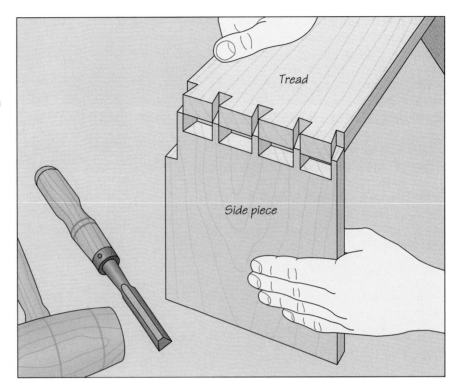

GLUING UP THE STEP STOOL

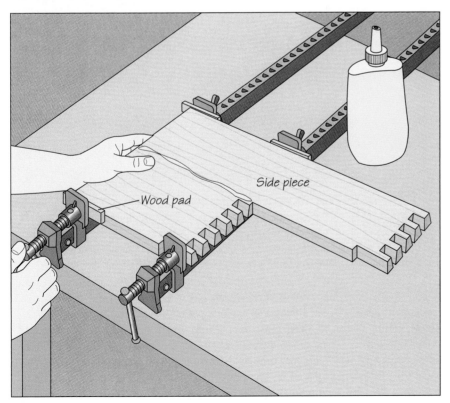

1 **Gluing up the sides**
Set a pair of bar clamps on a work surface and lay two boards that make up a complete side piece on them. Spread glue on the contacting edges of the boards, align their bottom ends, and tighten the clamps until there are no gaps between the boards and a thin bead of adhesive squeezes out of the joint *(left)*. Glue up the other side piece the same way.

2 Relieving the side pieces

By cutting a semicircle out of the side pieces, leaving two legs on each side, the stool will be more stable on uneven surfaces. Adjust a compass to a radius of 3½ inches and mark a semicircle on one of the side pieces, placing the compass point at the bottom end of the sides midway between the edges. Cut the semicircle on your band saw *(right)*, feeding the stock across the table with both hands. Then make the same cut on the other side piece. You can then smooth away the marks left by the saw blade on a spindle sander.

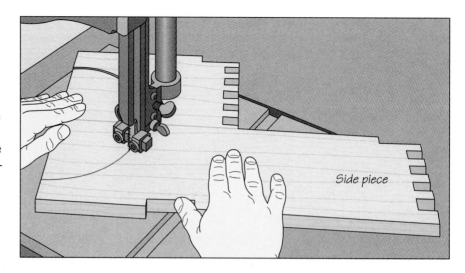

Side piece

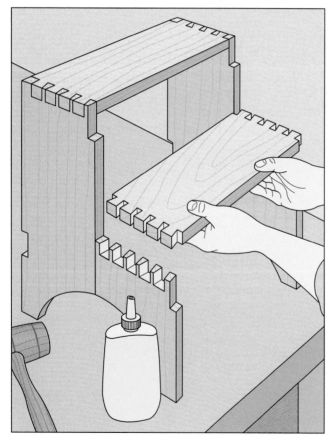

3 Installing the treads

Spread an even layer of glue on the contacting surfaces between the pins and tails, then assemble the stool, setting the treads on the side pieces *(above)*. Secure the joints with bar clamps, aligning the bars with the side pieces and using wood pads as long as the tread width to distribute the clamping pressure.

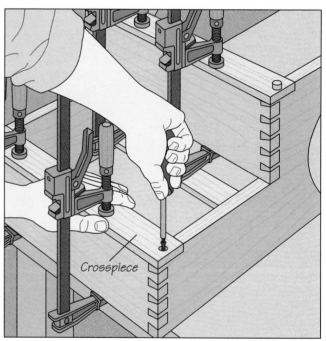

Crosspiece

4 Attaching the crosspieces

Set the step stool on its back edge and apply glue to the contacting surfaces between the crosspieces and the sides and treads. Place the crosspieces in their notches and clamp them securely in place. Near each end of the crosspieces, drill a counterbored hole for a wood screw through the crosspiece and into the front edge of the side piece. Drive a screw into each hole *(above)*. For a perfect match, use a plug cutter on your drill press to cut plugs from the waste wood left by relieving the side pieces *(step 2)*. Spread glue on the plugs and tap them into their holes, ensuring that the grain direction of each runs in the same direction as the crosspiece. Use a chisel to trim the plugs flush with the surface, then sand them smooth.

BUILDING A BOX KIT

First produced in the 1790s, Shaker boxes were made in graduated sizes to hold household goods; when empty, they could be nested inside one another. The oval boxes remain popular today, and can be made easily from commercial kits. The box shown at right was made by craftsman John Wilson of Charlotte, Michigan. He added a few luxurious refinements to the utilitarian yet elegant Shaker design, such as using bird's-eye maple for the box bands and a walnut burl veneer for the top.

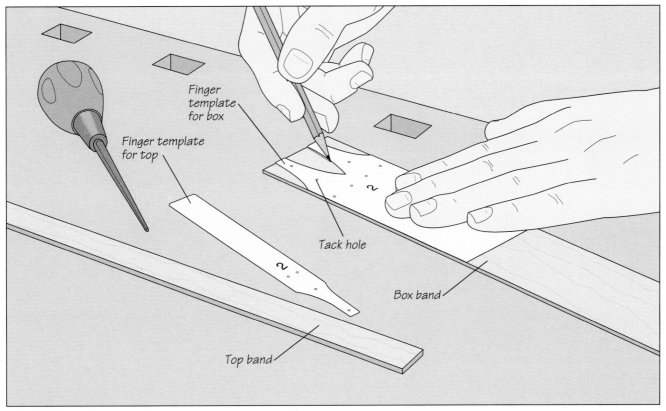

Finger template for box

Finger template for top

Tack hole

Box band

Top band

1 Cutting the fingers

To make a Shaker box from a commercial kit, first prepare the stock for the two bands—one for the box and one for the top. The bands are typically resawn from hardwood stock to a thickness of ⅟₁₆ inch. For best results, use straight-grained, quartersawn stock air-dried to a moisture content of 15 to 20 percent. Once the bands have been cut to size, use the proper-sized finger template to outline the fingers on the box band *(above)*, then mark the tack holes with an awl and drill them with a ⅟₁₆-inch bit.

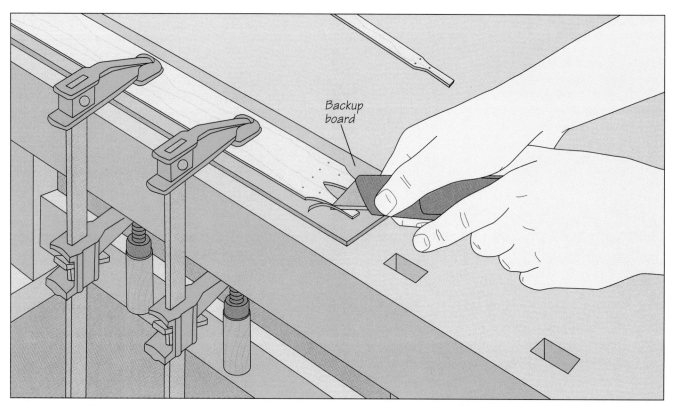

2 Beveling the fingers

Clamp the bands to a backup board and bevel the fingers with a utility knife. Holding the knife firmly with both hands, cut at an angle of 10° around the fingers *(above)*. Then taper the outside face of the opposite end of each band using a belt sander, starting the taper about 1½ inches in from the end. This will ensure a smooth overlap and uniform thickness once the bands are bent.

3 Marking the joint

Soak the box and lid bands in boiling water until they are soft—typically about 20 minutes. Remove the box band from the water and wrap it around the proper-sized box core so the beveled fingers lap over the tapered end. Make a reference mark across the edges of the band where the ends overlap *(right)*. Keep the beveled fingers pressed tightly against the core to prevent them from splitting.

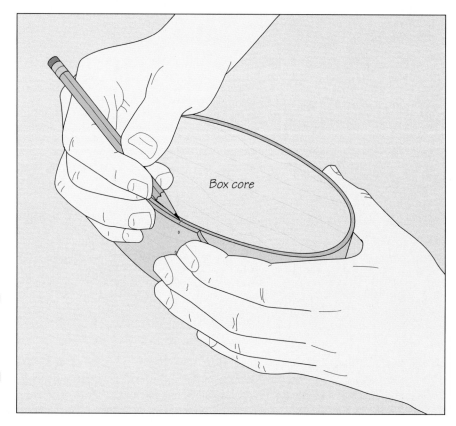

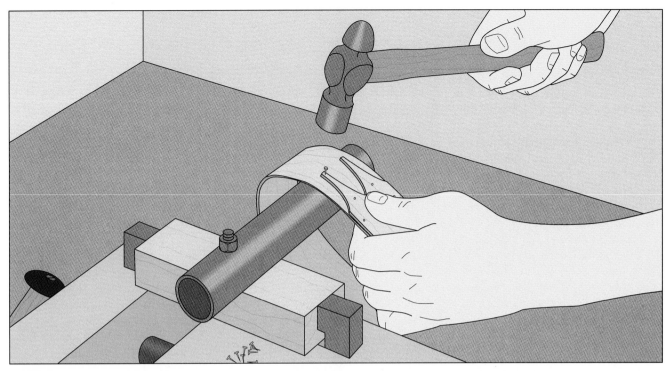

4 Tack-nailing the box
Working quickly, slip the band off the core, rebend it so that the pencil marks line up, and tack-nail it through the holes you drilled in step 1 using the appropriate copper tacks. To clinch the tacks inside the band, use a length of iron pipe clamped to your bench as an anvil *(above)*. Once the box bands are tack-nailed, place two shape-holders inside the band—one at each end—to maintain the oval form as it dries.

5 Shaping the lid band
Shape and tack-nail the top band for the box lid as described above, but use the drying box band as a bending form and shape-holder as it dries *(left)*. The fingers for the top and the box should line up evenly. Allow two days for the bands to dry. To complete the box, cut a lid and bottom from quartersawn stock to fit inside the bands, beveling the edges at 5° to provide a tight fit like a cork in a bottle. Then drill $\frac{1}{16}$-inch pilot holes and use toothpicks as pegs to secure the pieces. The boxes can be finished with milk paint or a clear lacquer.

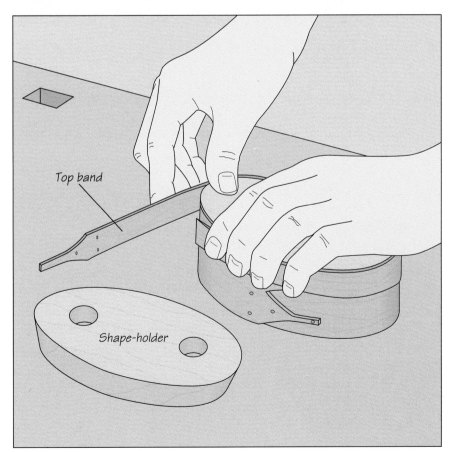

Top band

Shape-holder

PEGBOARD

"A place for everything and everything in its place" were words the Shakers lived by, and many household items in Shaker homes hung from assigned pegs.

The pegboard is a fitting symbol of the Shaker's approach to both daily life and craftsmanship. As with other Shaker-made items, the clean, unadorned lines of the pegboard reflected its humble function rather than any concern with appearance. But the simple design belied the pegboard's versatility. The boards did not just hold hats and coats. Lining the walls of Shaker homes, they were an integral part of household life—convenient, organized, and tidy, hangers for everything from bookshelves, pipe holders, and towel racks to candle sconces, chairs, clothes hangers (a Shaker invention), and wall clocks *(page 118)*.

For the modern woodworker, the pegboards also reveal the Shaker devotion to craft. The simple mushroom-shaped pegs were accorded the same attention to detail as the finest cabinet. For this reason perhaps, Shaker pegboards were remarkably consistent in design and construction no matter when or where they were made. The pegs were typically fashioned from maple or cherry and averaged 3 inches in length. They were secured to 3-inch-wide back boards usually mounted 6 feet above the floor. The spacing of the pegs varied according to the board's use. In New Lebanon and Hancock, the pegs were sometimes threaded and then screwed into the back board. Normally, however, they were attached with a friction fit, as described in this section.

You can buy pegs ready-made or turn them on your lathe. In either case, the base of the pegs will need to be kerfed to accommodate the wedges that secure them in place.

MAKING A PEGBOARD

1 Shaping the back board
Cut the back board to size from ⅞-inch-thick stock; make its width 3½ inches and its length dependent on the number of pegs you will mount. Shape the board on a router table using two different bits. Start by rounding over the front face of the board at the edges and ends *(page 120)*, then switch to a piloted bead bit. Align the fence with the bit's pilot bearing and adjust the cutting height so the beads will be about ½ inch from the edges of the board. To help you feed the workpiece, clamp a featherboard to the table, braced with a support board. Feed the back board into the bit on edge, keeping the front face pressed against the fence. Then turn the board over and repeat the procedure to rout the bead on the opposite edge *(right)*.

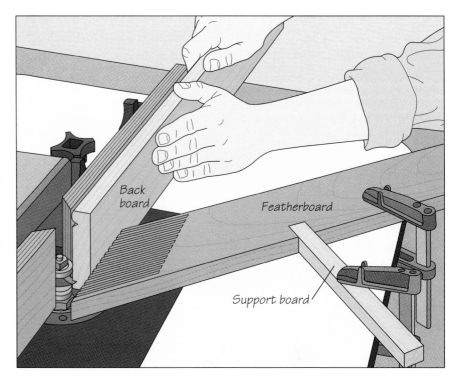

Back board

Featherboard

Support board

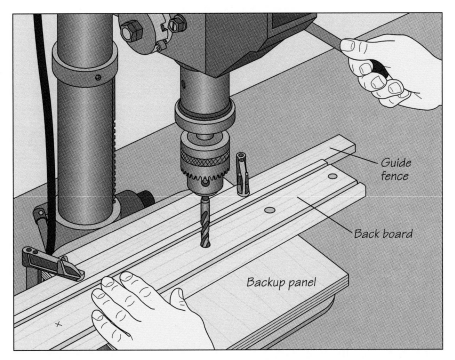

2 Preparing the back board for the pegs
Starting near one edge of the back board, mark the peg holes along the middle of the stock. (The pegs on the board shown at left will be spaced 5 inches apart.) Install a ½-inch brad-point bit in your drill press and attach a backup panel to the machine table to minimize tearout. Set the back board on the panel so the first mark is directly under the bit and clamp a board as a guide fence to the table flush against the workpiece. Then, butting the back board against the fence, drill the holes *(left)*.

Guide fence

Back board

Backup panel

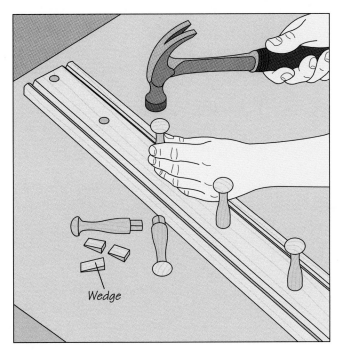

Wedge

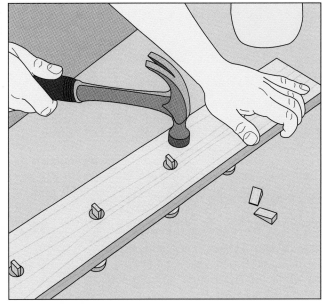

3 Tapping in the pegs
To make the pegs easier to install, use a sanding block to shape a small bevel around the base of each one. Then saw a kerf for a wedge across the base of the peg; to avoid splitting the wood with the wedge, make the cut at a right angle to the grain. Once the pegs are ready, spread glue on their bases and tap the pegs into the holes *(above)*.

4 Driving in the wedges
For each peg, cut a ⁷⁄₁₆-inch-long wedge from scrap wood. Spread glue in the kerfs and on the wedges, set the pegboard face down on a work surface, then tap the wedges in with a hammer *(above)*. Avoid using too much force; this may cause a peg to split. Trim the wedges flush with the back face of the board. Fasten the pegboard to the wall by counterboring screw holes and driving the screws into wall studs. Conceal the fasteners with wood plugs *(page 134)*.

GLOSSARY

A-B-C

Auxiliary fence: A wooden attachment to a tool's rip fence that serves as an anchor for accessories and prevents accidental damage to the metal fence.

Blank: A piece of solid or glued-up wood used to create a furniture part, such as a turned leg.

Bridle joint: A type of open mortise-and-tenon joint in which the tenon is as long as the width of the mortise piece and the mortise extends across the entire width of the board.

Candle sconce: A candlestick holder.

Chamfer: A bevel cut along the edge of a workpiece.

Cheek: The face of the projecting tenon in a mortise-and-tenon joint.

Clearance hole: A hole drilled in a workpiece to accommodate the shank of a screw.

Cleat: A strip of wood fastened to one furniture part to support another, such as a shelf or a tabletop.

Cockbeading: Narrow projecting molding surrounding the inside edge of the door opening of a cabinet.

Compound-angle hole: A hole drilled into a workpiece with the bit presented at angles other than 90° relative to the face and edge of the stock.

Corner strip: A notched wood block fastened to the stile of a cabinet or the rail of a table to hold up a shelf support or drawer slide.

Counterbore: Drilling a hole that permits the head of a screw or bolt to sit below a wood surface so that it can be concealed by a wood plug.

Countersink: Drilling a hole that permits the head of a screw or bolt to lie flush with or slightly below a wood surface.

Cross-dowel: A wood dowel or metal cylinder threaded across its axis to accommodate a screw or knockdown fastener; usually used to provide long-grain strength when screwing into end grain.

Crown molding: Decorative trim installed around the perimeter of a piece of furniture just below the top; also known as cornice molding.

D-E-F-G-H-I-J

Dado: A rectangular channel cut into a workpiece.

Edge gluing: Bonding boards together edge-to-edge to form a panel.

End grain: The arrangement and direction of the wood fibers running across the the ends of a board.

Fiber rush: A natural fiber made from the twisted leaves of cattails used to for seating material in chairs; a more commonly used alternative is made from twisted kraft paper.

Finial: An ornament—usually turned and carved—projecting from the upper corners of a furniture piece such as a chair.

Glass-stop molding: Decorative strips of wood used to hold a pane of glass in a door frame.

Half-blind dovetail: A dovetail joint in which the structure of the joint is concealed by one side; commonly used to join drawer fronts to the sides.

K-L-M-N-O-P-Q

Kerf: A cut made in wood by the width of a saw blade.

Kickback: The tendency of a workpiece to be thrown back in the direction of the operator of a woodworking machine.

Kicker: A board fastened across a drawer opening and positioned above the drawer to keep it from tilting down when opened.

Knockdown hardware: A fastener that allows the quick assembly and disassembly of a piece of furniture.

Leaf: A panel that is extended to increase the size of a table and retracted when not in use; it can be hinged or sliding.

Ledger strip: A short, narrow piece of wood used to support the top or bottom of a cabinet.

Listing: Canvas or woven wool cloth tape used for weaving chair seats; also known as Shaker tape.

Miter gauge: A device that slides in a slot on a saw or router table, providing support for the stock as it moves past the blade or bit; can be adjusted to different angles for miter cuts.

Molding: Decorative strips of wood used to embellish a piece of furniture.

Mortise: A hole cut into a piece of wood to receive a tenon.

Mortise-and-tenon joint: A joinery technique in which a projecting tenon cut in one board fits into a matching hole, or mortise, in another.

Mullion: A slim vertical member dividing sections of a frame; also known as a muntin.

Panel-raising plane: A hand plane with an angled sole used to bevel the sides of a panel in frame-and-panel construction.

Pilot hole: A hole drilled into a workpiece to prevent splitting when a screw is driven; usually made slightly smaller than the threaded section of the screw.

Pilot bearing: A free-spinning metal collar on a piloted router bit that follows the edge of a workpiece or a template to guide the bit during a cut.

Pommel: The square section left on a turned furniture leg; allows room for mortises needed to receive rails.

Push block or stick: A device used to feed a workpiece into a blade or cutter to protect the operator's fingers.

Quartersawn lumber: Wood sawn so the wide surfaces intersect the growth rings at angles between 45° and 90°; also known as vertical-grained lumber when referring to softwood.

R-S

Rabbet joint: A method of joining wood in which the end or edge of one workpiece fits into a channel, or rabbet, cut along the edge or end of another workpiece.

Rail: In a table, the rails join the legs and support the top; in a chair, one of four boards that frame the seat. Also the horizontal member of a frame-and-panel assembly. See *stile.*

Raised panel: In frame-and-panel construction, a cabinet or door panel with a bevel cut around its edges, a decorative effect that "raises" the center and allows the panel to fit into the groove cut in the frame.

Rake angle: The angle at which a chair leg deviates from the vertical when viewed from the side of the chair; see *splay angle.*

Rocker: The curved runners of a rocking chair joined to the chair legs.

Roughing gouge: A turning tool usually used to shape a square blank into a cylinder.

Rule joint: A pivoting joint commonly used in drop-leaf tables; features mating convex and concave profiles cut into the edges of the table leaf and top.

Shoulder: In a mortise-and-tenon joint, the part of the tenon that is perpendicular to the cheek.

Sliding dovetail joint: Similar to a tongue-and-groove joint, except the slide, shaped like the pin of a dovetail joint, is held by a mating groove.

Splay angle: The angle at which a chair leg deviates from the vertical when viewed from the front of the chair; see *rake angle.*

Stile: The vertical member of a frame-and-panel assembly. See *rail.*

Stopped dado: A dado that stops before crossing the full width or thickness of a workpiece.

Story pole: A shop-made measuring gauge used to determine the dimensions and the location of the joints in a project, such as a chair.

T-U-V-W-X-Y-Z

Tearout: The tendency of a blade or cutter to tear wood fibers.

Template: A pattern used to guide a tool in reproducing identical copies of a piece.

Tenon: A protrusion from the end of a workpiece that fits into a mortise.

Through dovetail joint: A method of joining wood by means of interlocking pins and tails, which pass entirely through the mating piece.

Tongue-and-groove joint: A joinery method featuring a protrusion from the edge or end of one board that fits into the groove of another.

Trestle: In a trestle table, a board running along the underside of the top to which the legs are attached.

Wood button: A small, square-shaped block with a rabbet at one end that fits into a groove; used to secure the top of a piece of furniture.

Wood movement: The shrinking or swelling of wood in reaction to changes in relative humidity.

INDEX

Page references in *italics* indicate an illustration of subject matter. Page references in **bold** indicate a Build It Yourself project.

ACKNOWLEDGMENTS

The editors wish to thank the following:

SHAKER DESIGN
James Archambeault, Lexington, KY; Elizabeth Fitzsimmons, Hancock Shaker Village, Pittsfield, MA;
Paul Rocheleau, Richmond, MA; June Sprigg, Pittsfield, MA

CHAIRS
Adjustable Clamp Co., Chicago, IL; American Tool Cos., Lincoln, NE; Black & Decker/Elu Power Tools,
Towson, MD; Connecticut Cane & Reed Co., Manchester, CT; Delta International Machinery/Porter-
Cable, Guelph, Ont.; Mike Dunbar, Portsmouth, NH; General Tools Manufacturing Co., Inc.,
New York, NY; Hancock Shaker Village, Pittsfield, MA; Hitachi Power Tools U.S.A. Ltd., Norcross, GA;
Ian Ingersoll, West Cornwall, CT; Jean-Pierre Masse, Montreal, Que.; Ryobi America Corp., Anderson, SC;
Sandvik Saws and Tools Co., Scranton, PA; Stanley Tools, Division of the Stanley Works, New Britain, CT

TABLES
Adjustable Clamp Co., Chicago, IL; Black & Decker/Elu Power Tools, Towson, MD;
Delta International Machinery/Porter-Cable, Guelph, Ont.; Great Neck Saw Mfrs. Inc.
(Buck Bros. Division), Millbury, MA; Les Realisations Loeven-Morcel, Montreal, Que.;
Ryobi America Corp., Anderson, SC; Sandvik Saws and Tools Co., Scranton, PA; Stanley Tools,
Division of the Stanley Works, New Britain, CT; Tool Trend Ltd., Concord, Ont.

PIE SAFE
Adjustable Clamp Co., Chicago, IL; American Tool Cos., Lincoln, NE; Robert Bourdeau, Laval, Que.;
Country Accents, Montoursville, PA; Delta International Machinery/Porter-Cable, Guelph, Ont.;
Great Neck Saw Mfrs. Inc. (Buck Bros. Division), Millbury, MA; Jean-Pierre Masse, Montreal, Que.;
Stanley Tools, Division of the Stanley Works, New Britain, CT; Tool Trend Ltd., Concord, Ont.;
Wainbee Ltd., Pointe Claire, Que./DE-STA-CO, Troy, MI

SHAKER CLASSICS
Adjustable Clamp Co., Chicago, IL; Atelier d'Ébénisterie Réjean Guerin Enr., St-Rémi, Que.;
Delta International Machinery/Porter-Cable, Guelph, Ont.; Great Neck Saw Mfrs. Inc. (Buck Bros.
Division), Millbury, MA; The Home Shop, Charlotte, MI; David Keller, Petaluma, CA; Murray Clock
Craft, Willowdale, Ont.; Sears, Roebuck and Co., Chicago, IL; Tool Trend Ltd., Concord, Ont.

The following persons also assisted in the preparation of this book:
Lorraine Doré, Solange Laberge, Geneviève Monette, Tim Reiman,
David Simon, Diana Von Kolken

PICTURE CREDITS

Cover Robert Chartier
6, 7 Steve Lewis
8, 9 Ed Homonylo
10, 11 Steve Lewis
12 James Archambeault
13 Courtesy Hancock Shaker Village
14, 15 James Archambeault (*both*)
16 Courtesy Hancock Shaker Village
17 Courtesy Hancock Shaker Village (*top*)
17 James Archambeault (*bottom*)
19 Paul Rocheleau Photography
20, 23, 39, 44 Courtesy Hancock Shaker Village